Early Childhood Education

*a review and discussion of
current research in Britain*

By Barbara Tizard

*Dr. Barnardo's Senior Research Fellow,
Thomas Coram Research Unit,
Institute of Education,
University of London*

*with comments by
Joan Tough
Marion Blank
Jerome Bruner
A. H. Halsey*

NFER Publishing Company

This book was first published by the Social Science Research
Council in 1974.
This edition is published by the NFER Publishing Company Ltd.,
Book Division, 2 Jennings Buildings, Thames Avenue,
Windsor, Berks SL4 1QS
Registered Office: The Mere, Upton Park, Slough, Berks SL1 2QD
This edition first published in 1975
© Social Science Research Council 1975
85633 076 0

Printed in Great Britain by
John Gardner (Printers) Ltd.,
Hawthorne Road, Bootle, Merseyside

Distributed in the USA by Humanities Press Inc.
Hillary House-Fernhill House, Atlantic Highlands,
New Jersey 07716 USA.

0036566

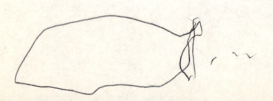

Contents

I would like to start by explaining how this review came to be written. In 1972 the government announced its intention to increase substantially the amount of educational provision for the under-fives, and to set up a research programme to monitor the development of the new provisions. In response to this announcement, the Social Science Research Council decided to increase its own expenditure in the pre-school area, and actively to commission research into key topics. As a first step in the process of identifying these topics, the SSRC invited me to review current research on pre-school education in the United Kingdom. From the start, the SSRC had in mind the desirability of mounting research that was not solely 'educational' in the narrow sense, but was concerned with the social and educational needs of the under-fives in a variety of settings. For this reason, and because of the obvious fact that most of the young child's learning occurs outside of school, I interpreted the terms of my commission rather broadly.

In writing the review, I tried to present as complete a report as possible of research which was being carried out in the field of early education in the UK. With very few exceptions, only work which was currently being carried out, or which had been completed but not yet published, was described. I did not include research concerned with handicapped children, with the exception of the rather substantial body of research being carried out with severely retarded children. It is unlikely that my coverage is complete, and I would like to apologize to anyone whose work was omitted. I think, however, that all the current major projects were included. Since the review was completed, the DES has given several new grants for research in this area; the details are listed at the end of Appendix II.

A number of people have criticized this review, on the grounds that by suggesting that nursery schools make no long-term difference to a child's development I have provided a justification for any local authority wanting to decrease its expenditure on early education. Such an inference would be quite unjustified, since it emerges very clearly from the review that what is needed is a considerable increase in both social and educational services for the under-fives and their families. It would, however, be foolish to justify such an increase by the argument that it will prevent later educational failure. There is considerable evidence that such an outcome is extremely unlikely. The justification for increased services must be the current needs of young children and their families. Starting from these needs, it does not follow that an expansion of the number of part-time nursery classes is the best way to meet them, and one of the functions which I hope this review will serve is to stimulate discussion about possible alternative forms of provision. Nor do I think it serves the best interests of children or teachers to take the present nursery school structure and curriculum as sacrosanct. A periodic re-thinking of goals and methods is desirable in every enterprise; in the case of nursery schools it can only be useful to examine the implicit assumptions of the system, and to raise the question of what is being learnt, and what is not being learnt, by the children who attend.

In order to increase the value of this book as a stimulant to discussion, the SSRC asked a number of people well-known for their work in early education to comment on specific topics in the review in which they have a particular interest. I am most grateful for their contributions.

The reader may like to know that the greater part of the money allocated by the Social Science Research Council for the initiation of research in the pre-school field was awarded to Professor Bruner in April 1975. In collaboration with Professor Harry Judge of the Oxford Department of Educational Studies, he proposes to set up a working seminar of academics, administrators, community activists and others concerned with the welfare and education of young children.

The plan is for a central core of between six and 10 participants, based in Oxford. Visitors will also be invited to join in the seminar from time to time. The research project begins in October and will continue for three years. The group will be known as the Oxford Pre-school Research Unit.

The seminar will work in three ways. First, they will study what is known about the social groups—family, neighbourhoods, peer groups —in which a child finds himself and how this affects his outlook and education. Secondly, they will look at how poverty affects children and, on the other hand, what sort of thing gives a child a flying start. Thirdly, they will look at different ways of intervening in families, communities and institutions to increase the support given to the pre-school child.

Barbara Tizard

Introduction

Settings for pre-school education

Education is never a process which occurs exclusively at school; for all children in our society much education occurs outside school (at home, in the street, from television, books) whilst much that goes on in school is not education. For young children this is particularly obvious, because formal schooling if it occurs at all occupies such a small part of their lives.[1] A child who attends a half-day nursery school from his third to his fifth birthday will have spent only about 4 per cent of the waking hours of the first five years of his life at school. Yet these are the years during which intellectual growth is most rapid. There is a further reason for viewing early education in a wider context, which relates to the particular characteristics of the nursery school. Even though structurally the nursery school is part of the formal education system, that is, part of a system which is deliberately organized by agencies outside the family for educational purposes, and takes place in a special setting, yet the curriculum and teaching methods in many ways resemble the informal education of the family. In this respect the nursery school differs markedly from the rest of the educational system. Primary and secondary schools are characterized by a curriculum not usually taught elsewhere—e.g. skills, such as reading and writing— and systematic instruction in bodies of knowledge, e.g. geography and physics. The teaching techniques used in such schools are very different from those used in the family, or in other informal learning situations. Instruction is almost exclusively verbal, it does not arise from a context of immediate events, and in so far as it is concerned with the mastery of symbol systems, it may indeed have no empirical referents (c.f. Bruner, 1972; Scribner and Cole, 1972).

By contrast, the curriculum of the nursery school can hardly be distinguished from that of the home. Joan Tough writes, 'Perhaps all

---

[1] The DES statistics for January 1973 showed that only 8.4 per cent of children aged 3–4 in England and Wales were attending nursery schools or classes, maintained and independent. (This figure excludes children in playgroups, day nurseries, or infant schools).

those of us who are concerned with the education of young children would endorse certain general objectives for the curriculum: that the child should gain physical skills, acquire a wide vocabulary, achieve control of the language system, learn to classify, be aware of temporal and spatial relationships, develop the concepts of number, acquire a range of general knowledge about the physical, biological and social world, become familiar with some stories, rhymes and music, be able to solve problems, express ideas in words, in pictures and through a variety of other materials, and develop an understanding of other people's needs and views' (Tough, 1975). But these skills and bodies of knowledge are learnt by almost all children at home, admittedly to varying degrees of excellence. Moreover, they are taught at home and at school by very similar methods. In contrast to the formal techniques used in schools for older children, instruction both at home and in nursery school occurs incidentally, and in the context of some ongoing experience. When symbols are introduced, they are taught with reference to the child's activity—e.g. numbers may be learnt by counting stairs. In both nursery school and home, play is the main activity expected of the child, even though a different meaning may be given to this activity by teachers and parents. In both settings the child is given considerable freedom to organize his own experiences and his activity is mainly self-chosen and self-directed.

This essential continuity between nursery school and home is recognized by most parents, who usually see the main benefit of nursery school attendance as social, that is the child is given the opportunity to mix with other children, and to get used to being looked after by a strange adult. 'Proper' learning they consider to start with primary school. Indeed, it may be argued that the main distinction between parents and pre-school teachers as educators is ideological—that is, both parents and teachers provide the same kind of learning experiences for the child, but the teacher formulates her objectives and has theories about her methods. It is, of course, an oversimplification to talk about the educational methods of 'Parents' as though they were an un-differentiated group. Clearly, transmission within the family varies in important ways with social class, education, and so on, but what I have tried to bring out here is the continuity between the educational experience of home and nursery school, compared with the dis-continuity between home and primary school.

Further, the educational distinction between nursery-school, playgroup and nursery[2] so crucial to the professional, is hardly apparent to the layman, who tends to refer to them all indiscriminately as either 'schools' or 'nurseries'. What *is* apparent is that in all these settings a wide range of play-equipment is provided, and the curriculum is essentially one of free play supplemented by stories and music. The fact that only in nursery school does the child play under the guidance of a trained teacher is a nicety whose significance is not widely understood or appreciated outside the teaching profession.

In whatever setting young children find themselves in our society, then, whether at home, in playgroups, with child-minders, in day nurseries or in nursery schools they are likely to be following a similar curriculum taught by similar methods, albeit more or less adequately. Pre-school education is certainly not something exclusive to the formal educational system, and this review will therefore not be restricted to a consideration of research in any one setting.

Background to the expansion of pre-school services

The occasion for this review was the government decision to increase the amount of school provision for the under-fives, and the subsequent decision by the DES and the SSRC to allocate research funds in this area. A marked expansion in the provision of care for the under-fives outside their families has recently occurred in many countries, apparently due to two rather distinct causes. In the first place, there is a growing reluctance on the part of women to accept the entire responsibility for the care of their young children; they may want to go out to work, or they may merely wish to be relieved of their children for a short period each day.

During the fifties and sixties Bowlby's theories of the dire consequences to young children of even a brief separation from their mothers acted as a constraint, at least amongst the middle-classes, to this tendency. But the constraint has faded with the growth of the

[2] In case the reader is also ill-informed these terms will be briefly explained. A nursery school is mainly staffed by trained teachers, and keeps ordinary school hours. Children attend either the morning or afternoon session or sometimes both. Playgroups are staffed by parents, nursery nurses or others without teaching training. They aim to provide the child with social and play experiences and usually offer either a morning or afternoon session. Nurseries are staffed by nurses or others without teacher training. They cater mainly for the children of working mothers, are usually open for a long day, and do not close for school holidays. All three types of provision may be maintained by the local authority or by a private person or group.

Women's Movement, and the widespread dissemination in some form of its ideas. At the same time, for a variety of social reasons, the informal substitute care arrangements previously used are becoming rarer. With populations more mobile, grandmothers less often live around the corner, whilst for the middle-class, nannies and domestic help have become scarce and expensive.

A quite separate reason for increased services for the under-fives is the widespread belief in government and administrative circles that the failure of many children within the school system is due to the shortcomings of their parents as pre-school educators. In the past, the limited scholastic success of working-class children was usually attributed either to the innate limitations of the children or to the fact that they were offered inferior educational opportunities—large classes, poor buildings, less well-educated teachers. However, a greater equalization of educational opportunity has not resulted in a levelling of academic achievement either in the West or in the Eastern European socialist countries, and research has increasingly stressed the relationship between school achievement and variables in the family rather than the school. Since it is known that by the age of seven there are marked social class differences in school achievement, the conviction has developed that those children who experience learning difficulties have been inadequately prepared for school by their parents. The expansion of pre-school facilities in the public sector is thus seen as a way of compensating for indifferent education in the private family.

These two rather distinct sources of pressure to provide care outside the family for the under-fives have led in the main to different forms of provision, and have been the subject of quite different amounts of research. Women's own attempts to shed some responsibility for child care have met with little governmental response; for the most part working-class women have had recourse to child minders, and middle-class women to parent-organized playgroups. Very little public money has been spent in this country on either provision or research into these services.

On the other hand, the hope of preventing school failure by intervention in the pre-school years has stimulated a limited amount of government spending on both provision and research. At the end of the sixties there was some increase in the state provision of nursery places, under the stimulus of the urban programme. The pre-school sector of the Educational Priority Area (EPA) programme was the largest action-research project mounted with this age-group, the British equivalent of 'Headstart' (Halsey, 1972). In five different regions of special need playgroups were started, or additional resources were put into existing nursery schools and playgroups. The traditional play-group or nursery school regimen was in many cases supplemented by special language or number programmes which lasted for one year, and were devised independently in each region to meet the requirements of the local teachers. In each region the children were tested at the beginning and end of the special programme. In some, but not all regions the children made significant gains on standardized language and/or number tests compared with control children who had followed the traditional nursery regimen. In addition, in the West Riding the children were re-tested with language tests at the end of their first year in primary school. Both those who had followed a special language programme in pre-school[3] and those who had attended traditional nursery schools increased their scores at the end of the year. For a number of reasons, including the increasing familiarity of the children with the tests, and the absence of a control group who had not attended pre-school, these findings are difficult to interpret. No assessment was made of the subsequent school attainments of the children who had attended EPA pre-school, although the main rationale of the project was the hope that skills would be developed which would increase success at primary school.

Although the EPA pre-school programme was completed by 1972, and thus falls outside the terms of reference of this review, some description of it is included because of its impact on subsequent developments. As a result of the EPA programme educational authorities were led to reconsider the adequacy of their provisions for the under-fives, nursery school teachers entered a debate which still continues about the adequacy of their traditional teaching methods, and research workers were led to reconsider the impact which early schooling on its own could have on children's achievements.

However, as the present review will show, at a time of considerable expansion in nursery education there is now very little ongoing re-search in Britain into the efficacy of either nursery education as such or of particular educational strategies within the school. The reasons for this will be discussed later. The greater part of British research with under-fives is concerned with other aspects of early development.

[3] In this report the term pre-school will be used to refer to any organized group provision for under-fives, whether nursery school, playgroup, or nursery.

I
Description of Current Research

1. Effects on children's achievements of attendance at nursery or playgroup, with or without a special language programme
There are only three major projects under way, or not yet published, to report. The most important is undoubtedly that carried out by H L Williams and colleagues of the National Foundation for Educational Research (NFER) in five Slough nursery schools. The aim of the study was to evaluate a programme designed to reduce failure in the primary school. The rationale was that school failure amongst disadvantaged children is related to their failure to acquire in their early years the basic repertoire of verbal, perceptual and conceptual skills and attitudes which are needed as a foundation for school success. It was hoped that the programme would present the children in a condensed form with the kind of experiences they were presumed to have missed at home. Stress was laid on both language and perceptual training. The project was thus similar in form and rationale to the research part of the EPA pre-school programme, and some of the schools were in an EPA area. However, much clearer answers emerged from the NFER study, mainly, perhaps, because there was a longer initial period of discussion with the schools, and because all the schools carried out the same programme.

A full year was spent in discussions with the teachers concerned, preparing and modifying the programme with their help. A modified version of the Peabody Language Development Kit (PLDK) was used, together with games for perceptual training. Small groups of children were taught with the PLDK for twenty minutes daily, and the nursery staff tried to reinforce the skills taught in these sessions at appropriate informal opportunities during the rest of the school day. Perceptual training with the children took the form of a graded series of games, which were conducted by nursery assistants under the supervision of the trained teachers. The experimental group was composed of 110 children; some had only one term of the programme before moving to primary school, others had up to six terms. All the children, together with a control group of 81 children in other nursery schools, were given an extensive battery of tests before starting on the programme and as they left it for primary school. The children were also followed up in the Primary School. At the end of their first term the Boehm Test of Basic Concepts and a measure of adjustment to school were administered. At the end of their sixth term assessments of attainments in reading and number were obtained.

The full report on this study is not yet available but some important findings have already emerged. The children in the programme made significant gains, compared to the control children who experienced a traditional nursery programme, on the Illinois Test for Psycho-linguistic Abilities (ITPA) language battery and some of the perceptual tests. However, with the exception of the Verbal Expression sub-test of the ITPA, which is essentially a test of verbal fluency, the children who had spent only two terms in the programme made gains as large as those who had spent four or more terms. The social class gap in test scores was not closed, because children in all social classes made gains of a similar size. But when tested at the age of seven there were no significant differences between the school attainments of the control children and those who had taken part in the programme. Moreover, teachers' ratings during the second half of the first term at primary school showed no difference in personal, emotional, or social adjust-ment, between children who had attended either type of nursery school and children without any nursery school experience.

Williams has recently started a new project with pre-school children, which will compare the cognitive styles of children from advantaged and disadvantaged homes. A battery of tests is being devised to measure learning ability, reasoning and analytic style, controlling mechanisms, perceptual and language development, self-concept and motivation to achieve. The second stage of the project will evaluate the success of a series of games aimed to train the child in good thinking techniques and in the analytic use of language.

In Scotland, Margaret Clark and Carol Lomax of Strathclyde University have undertaken an evaluation of the effectiveness of the nursery schools recently set up by the Dunbartonshire Education Committee. The research design involved comparing the children of three consecutive years' intake to two primary schools. The children were tested in their first and second term at primary school, and at the end of each school year during the first three years of school. None of the first year's intake had attended nursery school; about a half of the second year's intake and three-quarters of the third year's intake had attended nursery school for at least one year. The children came from a fairly stable working-class community, and only one nursery school was involved (the first one to be opened in the county). The headmistress of the nursery school placed some stress on the development of cognitive skills, and the half-day programme included besides free-play a thirty-minute period in small groups when the children were encouraged to concentrate on some task chosen to help language or concept development. The children were tested with a large battery of verbal and non-verbal tests in the first term of primary school; thereafter reading tests were used in the follow-up study. The results are not yet available, and interpretation of them may be complicated by staff changes in the primary schools concerned.

Nikolas Rose, on behalf of the National Society for Prevention of Cruelty to Children, is carrying out a longitudinal study of 100 children in ten 'therapeutic' playgroups. These are playgroups for children referred by NSPCC caseworkers, usually because the family is under some stress, for psychiatric and/or financial or housing reasons, or because the child is in possible danger. All the children in the study had been recently admitted to a playgroup, within three months of their third birthday. Twenty children on the books of social workers, but not attending a playgroup, serve as controls. All the children are being assessed with the following measures: (1) the English Picture Vocabulary Test; (2) a specially devised comprehension of syntax test, which involves showing an understanding of language by moving toys to instruction; (3) spontaneous speech samples in two situations, i.e. playing with an adult, who takes a non-directive role, and in a respondent role with an adult; (4) a test of understanding of number; (5) a perceptual motor co-ordination test, developed from a number of other scales; (6) a modified version of the Rutter Scale; (7) an interview about the child's behaviour problems with the mother; (8) questions to the mother on her use of language with the child. This assessment is to be repeated every six months for two years. Nikolas Rose also wants to look at how much time each child spends in various activities in the playgroup, and how much time he spends interacting with other children, on his own, and with the play leader.

The paucity of projects in this section probably reflects the fact that most research workers by now consider that the simpler questions about the influence of nursery school attendance on children's achievements have been answered. Numerous American studies, the EPA project and the very thorough NFER study, appear to have established (i) that the ordinary playgroup or nursery school regimen, unsupplemented by special staff ratios or support systems for the staff, has no significant effect on children's test scores or primary school achievements; (ii) that by the end of the first term of primary school the general adjustment and classroom behaviour of children who have attended playgroup or nursery school does not differ from that of children who have not had this experience; (iii) that if special measures designed to improve children's cognitive skills are introduced into playgroups or nursery schools, then provided that the staff are enthusiastic in carrying them out there are significant increases in the test scores of the children who take part; (iv) children from all social classes make gains of about the same magnitude, so that unless the special help is restricted to children who are considered in special need the social class gap in achievement is not narrowed; (v) the increases in test scores occur very quickly; we do not know whether they are due to a generalized increase in cognitive skills and knowledge or to an admittedly valuable greater ease and familiarity with the question and answer situation gained in the course of the programme; (vi) unless special measures are taken to continue individualized help with the child once he has entered primary school the gains made in pre-school 'wash out' and his school achievements are unaffected by his pre-school experiences.

In so far, then, as the expansion of early schooling is seen as a way of avoiding later school failure or of closing the social class gap in achievement, we already know it to be doomed to failure. It would perhaps be sensible for research workers to point this out very clearly to public authorities at an early stage. This is not, of course, to say that such an expansion has no value—no one would agree that a young child should not be fed well, because his present diet may not affect his adult weight and height. Nursery schooling, or particular forms of it, may help to develop the child's social and cognitive skills as well as add to the happiness of both child and mother. What seems certain, however, is that without continuous reinforcement in the primary school or home, pre-school education has no long-term effect on later school achievement. Acknowledgement of this fact by many research workers has resulted in a re-direction of inquiry in several directions, which will now be reviewed. Even if, without continuing reinforcement, long-term improvement in children's cognitive skills can't be affected, the question of what and how to teach young children remains. What can a child of three or four learn? How can we best develop his cognitive skills? Three British projects, all supported by the Schools Council, are concerned with these questions.

2. The development of special curricula or educational strategies for use in pre-schools

Joan Tough, in Leeds, is currently organizing a curriculum project entitled 'Communication skills in early childhood'. This is one of the very few curriculum or compensatory projects to be derived from a prior study of development. The study in question was a longitudinal investigation of language development in middle and working-class children, much influenced by the work of Basil Bernstein (Tough, 1973). Joan Tough found that even at the age of three there were differences in both the linguistic structure and language functions of middle- and working-class children. The working-class children less often used language to report on past experiences or to predict the future, to give explanations, justify behaviour, and reflect on feelings. In addition, their mean length of utterance was shorter and their sentence structure was less complex. However, at the age of seven when language was recorded in a greater variety of situations it became clear that in certain situations, e.g. conversation with their peers, the working-class children could, and did, produce as long and complex utterances as middle-class children. But the purposes for which they used language still appeared to be different. In particular, working-class children tended not to be explicit—they seemed to assume that the listener shared their viewpoint; they tended to reflect less on their own past experiences and to use these less in accounting for the immediately observable present.

Joan Tough concluded that the educational problem is not to teach working-class children to talk more often, or in longer or more complex sentences, since all the linguistic structures are available to them if they choose to use them. The problem is rather that they have had little practice in using language for certain purposes. In professional families the mother encourages the child to make comparisons, to recall the past, and to anticipate the future, to offer explanations, and look for differences; she reads him stories, encourages creative indoor activities and imaginative play. Because the working-class child has had much less of these kinds of experience he enters school with a different set of meanings, and does not respond in the way which the teacher hopes to the tasks she sets him. Her response is usually to decide that his 'language is poor' and to try to extend his vocabulary and syntax; what he needs, however, is help in the development of verbal thinking skills. This rationale underlies Joan Tough's curriculum development research.

A year was spent with a working party of teachers preparing a draft guide entitled 'Listening to Children Talk'. This is now being used with 80 groups of teachers all over the country, in all involving about 1,500 teachers. The project depends on a very complex organization, with five full-time staff, and conferences in Leeds and in each region from time to time with head teachers, class teachers, and representatives of education authorities. The first phase of the study is aimed to make teachers more aware of the way in which the young child uses language, what features to listen for, how and when to listen, and how to appraise and make records of children talking. Each group of teachers play and discuss a series of six videotapes, and after each one try out the suggested techniques in their schools, then return and discuss as a group their findings. It is planned to evaluate the success of the project in altering teachers attitudes to children's language at the final meeting of the first year. At this session the teachers will be asked to comment on the final videotape, and their discussion will be tape-recorded and analysed. The second phase of the project, 'Fostering Children's Language', will be carried out in the same way, but during this year ways of helping children to use language more effectively will be suggested. The essential technique which will be recommended involves the teacher entering into dialogue with the child. This, then, is no 'teacher-proof' language programme, but an attempt to bring in to the school in a systematic way the language teaching techniques of the middle-class mother, and to use them with children who have little experience of such techniques. The teachers are to be encouraged not simply to listen to the child with interest or to 'chat' with him, but to help the child to ask questions, solve problems, explore the meaning of particular situations, and in general to use language as a means of learning.

A second project, of particular interest because of its unusual subject matter, is one concerned with music education of young children, directed by Arnold Bentley and Iain Kendell at Reading. Although this project is being carried out in primary schools, it is included in this review because the work began in nursery schools and is intended to be used with children from the age of four. An attempt is being made to devise equipment and material for the musical education of young children in the classroom. The aim of this education is to lead children towards musical literacy, so that by the age of 10 or 11, they can decode a simple tune, play a simple instrument like the glockenspiel, and improvise and if possible write down their own tunes. To these ends Iain Kendell is devising a structured programme which will help develop basic musical skills, such as auditory discrimination. This programme, which includes musical games of various kinds, e.g. musical dominoes, is being developed so that it can be used by two or three children at a time in the classroom, whilst the other children are busy with other tasks. Because the programme is devised for the use of the ordinary class teacher, rather than a music specialist, it calls for little technical knowledge on her part. Hence each musical exercise comes with exact instructions and a statement of its aims. Much use is made of relatively child-proof material such as cassette tape-recorders, glockenspiels, and drums.

The programme, which at the moment is being developed in a few pilot schools, will be used in 40 trial schools in the main study. One hundred and sixty further schools will use the material and send in reports. It is hoped to pre- and post-test a sample of the children in the trial schools for such skills as the ability to keep a steady pulse, reproduce a rhythm, reproduce a melodic phrase, decode music symbols and understand such musical concepts as fast and slow. It is planned to get evaluations of the programme from the class teachers, head teachers, music advisers and the observations of the Project Team. Iain Kendell thinks that it is not enough to help children to enjoy music—they can enjoy it much more if they develop musical skills and literacy. In fact, young children have more musical skills than they are usually given credit for—at the age of four most can distinguish minims and crotchets, and even at this age can readily be taught to use musical terminology.

A third curriculum project, on Early Mathematical Experiences, is directed by Geoffrey and Julia Matthews at the Centre for Science Education, Chelsea College. The aim of the project is to study relevant experiences in the nursery school which may help in the development of children's mathematical ideas, and to help teachers with suggestions for encouraging such activities. The project will last for three years, and during this period it is hoped to assemble and try out a Teacher's Guide. This will describe the network of mathematical concepts which the young child acquires during development and make suggestions for teachers about how to facilitate their emergence and use.

As in Joan Tough's Communication Skills project, the key to the project organization is the establishment of local groups of teachers who will pool their experiences, make observations, identify the best current practices, and help to draw up and try out the Teacher's Guide. Twenty-two working groups of teachers have been formed, and in addition 30 'associate' groups will try out ideas. Two nursery teachers seconded to the Project will visit the groups, visit nursery classes, and try out ideas themselves within schools.

All three projects described above are essentially concerned with curriculum development and teacher sensitization; evaluation of the effectiveness of the curricula in increasing children's achievement is either not included, or occupies a very minor position in the project, because of the large amount of time and resources which would be entailed in an adequate evaluation. Aside from these major projects, there appear to be very few studies of teaching strategies in the pre-school and of their effectiveness, although these would appear to be the kind of studies that could be carried out on a small scale in Colleges of Education. An interesting exception is an attempt by Carol Lomax of Strathclyde University to determine the short-term effects of story-telling in the nursery school on children's vocabulary. Vocabulary was tested before and after storytelling. The results suggest that whether or not a child learned new words was related not to whether the teacher had explained the words during the course of the story, but to whether during the telling the child had participated and appeared to be interested. In this study an attempt was made to determine whether a particular educational strategy, storytelling, had the effect which the teacher intended of increasing the children's vocabulary. Pre- and post-testing was carried out with specially devised measures, rather than standardized tests, and the educational process was observed to collect further evidence on the important variables in learning. Many more studies of this kind are needed.

Ken Jones, of Redland College, Bristol, has recently carried out a pre-reading research project with four-year-old children in Bristol play-groups. Twenty-four children in a number of different playgroups were given three 20-minute sessions a week for a term with the Peabody 'rebus' programme. This programme attempts to teach pre-reading skills. Six months later, after one term in Infants School, their scores on a test of basic skills involved in reading were significantly higher than those of children who had followed the Peabody Language Development Programme for one term, or those who had been shown new play materials during sessions of equivalent duration. It is not known, however, whether the reading attainments of the 'rebus' taught children differed from those of the others. Jones is now preparing a revised version of the rebus material, which will be more suitable for English children and involve the use of less expensive material.

3. Analysis of factors affecting staff behaviour in the pre-school

American investigators have tended to ascribe cognitive gains in the pre-school to the effects of the special instructional programmes introduced and have shown little interest in staff behaviour during the rest of the school day. This seems related to a certain lack of faith on their part in pre-school teachers, who are often suspected of merely child-minding when they are not carrying out a scripted programme. Hence there has been a tendency to develop 'teacher-proof' material and to ignore staff–child interactions not scripted by a psychologist. However, because virtually all studies have relied on pre- and post-testing and have not monitored staff–child interactions either during the special sessions or during the rest of the school day, we do not know the relative importance of these periods. In fact it seems reasonable to suppose that the way in which staff talk to children will alter if they become enthusiastic about a language programme, and it may well be this alteration, rather than the programme *per se*, which brings about an improvement in the child's language skills. Such an effect would explain the fact that a variety of apparently dissimilar approaches have an equivalent effect in increasing children's achievements (Weikart, 1972). It would therefore seem important, especially for those responsible for staff training, to examine the processes going on within the school, to see whether the children's achievements can be related to the minute-to-minute characteristics of staff behaviour, and to study the factors which affect staff behaviour. From an administrative point of view it is also important to know whether there are clear advantages to the employment of teachers rather than nursery nurses; for the College of Education, it is important to know whether beliefs and attitudes about education do indeed influence the way in which staff behave.

In a study by Barbara Tizard and Janet Philps (Thomas Coram Research Unit, London) observations on staff behaviour were made in 12 different pre-school centres. Four were nurseries rather than schools, and the staff, who were not teachers, disclaimed any educational aim; four were traditional nursery schools, and four were nursery schools which had departed from tradition to the extent of including a special language programme in the school day. In half of the centres most of the children had parents in the manual working-classes, whilst in the other half the parents of the children were predominantly from the professional middle-classes.

The results (Tizard, Philps and Plewis, in press) show that significant differences did occur in staff behaviour in the various types of centres. In those nursery schools where a language programme was used the staff spent more time interacting with the children, rather than merely supervising them or putting out play equipment. In the nursery centres which had no avowed educational aim there was least talk addressed to the children, the lowest amount of information was given, the fewest suggestions for activities were made, and the least time was spent explaining or showing children how to do things. Further, all types of 'cognitive' staff behaviour, as well as total amount of talk to children were observed more often in middle-class than working-class centres, whilst in working-class centres the staff spent more time putting out equipment and merely supervising the children. Thus, the greatest 'cognitive' content in staff behaviour was found in the middle-class schools with a language programme, the least in the working-class nurseries not staffed by teachers.

For whatever reasons (and there are almost certainly complex interactions involved), those children whose verbal skills most needed extending were receiving the least extension, whilst the most verbally gifted children were receiving the most language teaching. It seems clear that very deliberate planned positive discrimination by teachers is needed to reverse this tendency. Further, there was considerable evidence that the beliefs of the staff about the function of the centre influenced their behaviour—in those centres where the staff saw their main function as looking after children whilst their mothers worked, or providing them with an opportunity to play with other children, the staff interacted less with the children and in a more supervisory capacity than did staff in centres with avowedly educational aims.

However, although there was clear evidence that the way in which the staff behaved was affected by the social class of the children they were looking after, and by their beliefs about the function of the centre, it was less clear that staff behaviour in fact affected the children's achievements. All the mean test scores of the middle-class children were higher than those of the working-class groups, and within each social class the quality of staff behaviour in the different types of centre did not appear to affect test scores, with one exception—the working-class children attending nursery schools with special language programmes had significantly higher language scores than the other working-class children. There are too many uncontrolled variables in this study for the findings to be definitive, but it provides a useful reminder that altering teachers behaviour does not necessarily result in altering children's achievements in the expected way. What is learnt often differs from what is taught.

Asher Cashdan (The Open University) is currently piloting, with Janet Philps, a study of teacher effectiveness in the nursery school. The aim of the main study will be to observe the practice of a wide variety of teachers, and to relate differences between what teachers do to differences in the behaviour of the children in their charge. His criterion of effectiveness is a short-term outcome, which he will assess not in terms of scores on standardized tests or skill acquisition but rather in terms of the effectiveness with which the child uses the school environment. He will therefore develop measures to assess the way in which the child uses the adults as a resource, the ways in which he uses the materials provided by the school, and the level of his play and of his peer interactions. The teachers' behaviour will be assessed by observation in the school setting and in a structured situation. In the school setting, time sampling schedules will be used and verbal interactions with the children will be recorded. Cashdan will look to see who initiates the interaction, how complex in content and structure the teacher's speech is, and to what extent the teacher builds on the children's utterances, and helps them to develop and clarify their meanings. In addition, the teacher's interactions with the child will be assessed in a standardized one-to-one situation, when she is asked to work with the child using a toy zoo. This latter situation may also be used in a similar way with the child and his mother. This would provide material which would help to answer an important question, that is as to whether the child's mother and his teacher talk to him in different ways, and whether he sees them as different kinds of person. A mismatch between school and home may have important consequences for the child's ability to learn from the school environment.

4. The influence of a variety of social factors on child behaviour in the pre-school

The point was made earlier that the traditional psychologist's approach of intervening in the child's life by providing, e.g. nursery school experience or a particular instructional programme, and assessing the effectiveness of the intervention by standardized tests administered before and after the event, is often very uninformative. If the child's scores have improved we do not usually know whether there has been any real change in his cognitive skills or whether he has merely gained more experience in responding in a question and answer situation. Even if one assumes that a real cognitive growth has occurred one does not know which aspect of what was probably a very complex intervention was effective. If the child's scores do not improve, it may be that changes have none the less occurred in the child, but one has not developed adequate measures of the changes. Consequently, the interest of many psychologists has turned from 'product testing' to an investigation of processes. What evidence is there in the child's spontaneous language and play of the level at which he is functioning, of what he is learning, and of how various aspects of the school situation impinge on him?

Barbara Tizard and Janet Philps observed 132 children aged three and four years in 12 pre-school centres. The play behaviour of the children was categorized in a number of ways, and their social interactions and conversations were recorded. There was no overall difference between middle-class and working-class children with respect to the complexity or duration of their play sequences, but symbolic play was observed more often in middle-class children. The play interests of children of different social class differed in a number of ways: working-class children more often preferred to play with trucks and tricycles and large constructional equipment such as boxes and tyres, and they more often preferred to play outside. This preference for outdoor play did not depress their level of play. On the contrary, when outdoors the working-class children's play sequences were more complex than when they were inside; they were also longer than those of the middle-class children either indoors or out. Indoors the working-class children tended to flit from one activity to another and to make very inadequate use of the play material provided. This finding suggests that the complaint that working-class children have a poor attention-span, or cannot concentrate, is a function of the situation rather than the child. The educational problem is less one of improving their concentration, than of motivating them inside the classroom, or of evolving educational strategies to use outside the classroom. There was no difference in the frequency with which working-class and middle-class children talked to their peers or to the staff; the nature of the interactions is currently being analysed. The main sex differences observed were in choice of play material (girls more often played on the climbing frame and swings than boys, and more often played with 'home corner' equipment) and in the level of peer interaction—girls more often achieved a high level of co-operation in play than boys. There were complex interactions between the effects of social class and type of centre on play.

In this study play was considered mainly as witness to the cognitive functioning of the children in a spontaneous, non-test bound situation. Just as an adult's conversation and actions in a variety of contexts bear witness to the quality of his intellectual functioning, so play, which is the characteristic mode of functioning of young children, tells us a great deal about their cognitive level. A caveat which must be entered is that play, like language, is probably situation-dependent; the play of a child in the primary school playground is different from his play at home, and it is likely that play in nursery school too differs in important ways from play at home.

Another aspect of play which is important for education is not as a marker of cognitive level, but as a learning process. Nursery school ideology lays great stress on play as the most important way in which the child learns. It seems clear, however, that in much play no learning occurs, or at the most one would guess that the child was over-learning some well rehearsed skill. On the other hand, much of what the child learns does not come from the medium of play but, e.g. from conversation with adults. We know very little about what kinds of play are necessary for what kinds of learning. A research programme which is just starting under the direction of John and Corinne Hutt at Keele University will focus on this question. Four problems have been selected for inquiry. The first problem concerns what the pre-school child actually does, and how this may vary in the different settings, i.e. nursery school, nursery class, playgroup or day-nursery. Data from the child at home are already being collected. This study will also obtain information about the variety and duration of activities elicited by different types of material, e.g. sand, paint, clay, and also the total amount of attention paid to these materials. Age differences in activity patterns and in attention spans will be examined. The second question will be an investigation of what children may be learning from their play, by the use of experimental toys, tests of transfer, etc. The third study will be concerned with the role of the adult in the child's activity.

The questions to which answers will be sought are as follows: (a) Do adults intervene or interact more frequently in certain types of children's activities than in others? (b) Do the frequency and nature of adult participation differ in the context of the nursery school, the playgroup, and the day-nursery? (c) How much of the adult's participation is requested by the child and how much is initiated by the adult herself? (d) What is the effect of the adult's intervention—does the child's activity cease or change, does it promote further active inquiry or verbal dialogue, and with what frequency do these consequences occur? The fourth study will explore the nature of individual differences in play and exploration and examine their educational implications, e.g. Do girls seek more verbal information than boys? Performances in problem-solving tasks will be examined in the context of the mother's instructional procedure, as well as that of a teacher or nursery nurse. Attention will be given to the strategies a child adopts and how these may be modified by an adult's intervention.

Kevin Connolly and Peter Smith at Sheffield University have used experimental methods to study the effects of variations in staff behaviour on the behaviour of children in a playgroup. With one group of 24 children the staff were asked to maximize their interactions and involve themselves in the children's activities; the behaviour of the children in this situation was compared with that of a second group of 24 with whom the staff were asked to interact to a minimal extent. In the latter group, there was a higher rate of social interactions between children, i.e. talking, object exchange, rough-and-tumble play, fantasy play. Results for aggressive behaviour, and for tests of cognitive and language ability at the beginning and end of the project were rather inconclusive.

In a second study the effect of variations in the size of the groups—which varied from 12 to 30 children—on the children's behaviour was investigated. This study is still in progress. Observations were also made of the spontaneous speech of children and staff in the normal language environment of the playgroup. These were related to the verbal interactions of mothers and their children in a series of tasks both in the home and at the playgroup. The measures of speech included quantitative analyses, accounts of form and range of functions. It was found that in the playgroup with maximal staff intervention there was more child speech related to action, rather than information, than in the playgroup with minimal staff intervention. However, in both groups speech relating to action was addressed more to other children, whilst that relating to information was addressed more to adults. Other results show that there were more child utterances in the playgroup with maximal staff intervention, and more utterances within this group were directed to adults rather than children. Older children and boys spoke more to other children than to adults. Staff, though varying in patterns of speech, tended to elicit a large proportion of one word responses, certain discernable patterns evoking predictable responses. Tasks set for the mothers produced predicted differences in mean length of utterance; simple descriptive tasks for instance, produced a longer mean length of utterance than more complex ones involving propositional terms. These analyses are presently being refined and extended for application to observations made in the study involving group size differences. Longer sequences of discourse are being recorded with a view to investigating effectiveness in initiation and sustainment of topics in conversation.

5. Studies of the effect of physical environmental variables on child behaviour in the pre-school

Although large amounts of public money are being spent on building in connection with the nursery school expansion programme, we know very little about the importance of the physical environment for the educational process. Do size and layout matter, and if so, in what way? How important is it to provide a wide range and variety of play equipment? Is it possible that children learn certain things more effectively, or that they are happier, in small domestic houses rather than open plan purpose-built schools?

Kevin Connolly and Peter Smith have recently attempted an experimental investigation of some of the variables. They looked at the effect of varying the supply of toys and the amount of space available on the behaviour of children in an experimental playgroup. The main effect of increasing the amount of available space was an increase in free motor behaviour, especially running and chasing; there was little or no effect on the kind or amount of social interaction between the children. Varying the supply of play equipment had a more important social effect: when this was reduced there was more sharing of toys, larger groups were formed, there was more aggressive behaviour and more signs of stress, e.g. thumb sucking and inactivity.

An observational approach to the same problems is being made in a study directed by Rudolf Schaffer and Tom Markus in Glasgow. This study aims to relate types of child and staff behaviour important to the educational and social aims of the institution to features of the building design. Children and staff will be observed in the schools and nurseries and their behaviour recorded in ethologically based categories. A semi-structured interview will be used to elicit from staff their views of what is done and what they think should be done in the institution and how they are influenced by the building in which they work. The staff's view of what happens obtained from these interviews will be compared with what actually happens as recorded observationally. Aspects of the buildings themselves such as lighting, surveillance features, etc., will also be measured directly. Particular attention will be paid to behaviour concerned with use of space, relationships of children to their peers and to adults, type of activity and attention span, disruptive and anti-social behaviour, etc. It is hoped that this work will complement the experimental work of Smith and Connolly.

6. Non-cognitive aspects of children's behaviour in nursery school

The research of Margaret Manning, at Edinburgh, stands almost alone, concerned as it is with entirely non-cognitive aspects of children's behaviour in the pre-school. In an earlier study she established categories of hostile behaviour in nursery school children, and from this standpoint 'typed' children according to their dominant mode of aggression. She describes four types of children, grouped according to the relative proportion of each type of behaviour. Group 1 children are unusually timid and unassertive in their usual social relationship, but become wild, excited and rough in games. Group 2 children are the 'teasers'; their hostility is not provoked by the immediate situation but seems aimed to provoke a reaction from another child, often one child repeatedly. Group 3 children are characterized by 'teasing' but also by specific hostility, that is, hostility provoked by a specific situation, e.g. a property dispute. Group 4 children are mainly characterized by 'specific' hostility. These groups of children differ in other characteristics. The Group 4 'specifically hostile' children are more verbal than the others, more friendly, make the most suggestions, orders and invitations. Group 2 children, the teasers, use the highest proportion of hostile speech and tend to win disputes.

At present Margaret Manning is engaged in a follow-up study of children categorized in this way at the age of three or four, who are now seven to eight. She is also extending the typing method to a further group of 60 pre-school children, with the aim of considering the influence on hostility type of social class, sex, family size and position in family.

RESEARCH CONCERNED WITH YOUNG CHILDREN AT HOME

Up to this point the research projects discussed have been more or less directly concerned with aspects of the formal educational system (as defined on p. viii), that is, with the provision or evaluation of educational strategies or services, or with the analysis of factors affecting the behaviour of staff and children within these settings. However, as was pointed out at the beginning of this review, most of what is learnt by the young child is learnt at home. It is at home, or in the neighbourhood, that he acquires not only most of his stock of knowledge but also strategies for relating to peers and to adults and strategies of learning. Moreover, because of the strong emotional links with his family it is from his family that the child learns the kind of adult behaviour to emulate and the kind of children's activities which are highly regarded.

7. Parent education programme

It is considerations such as these, together with disappointment with the results of remediation programmes in nursery schools and play-groups which have led a number of investigators to conclude that children's achievements will only be improved if parents can be helped to become more effective pre-school educators. To this end, parent education programmes have been devised. Two assumptions underlie this strategy. Firstly, it is assumed that working-class parents, or at any rate those whose children subsequently have learning difficulties at school, fail to provide their young children with certain essential experiences, or perhaps provide an excess of confusing experiences, e.g. too much unintelligible television. Secondly, it is assumed that their child-rearing methods can be fairly readily changed when alternative methods are explained to them.

However, we have very little knowledge at even the most superficial level of the learning environment of young children at home, and which aspects of their environment are significant for later scholastic achievement. It seems likely that sometimes false inferences about the child's home environment and out-of-school behaviour are drawn from his behaviour at school. Some investigators have found that children who in their first term at school appear almost mute, and unable to use a pencil, are talkative and competent in out-of-school settings. Douglas Hubbard, at Sheffield, before setting up a parent education programme, made a study of 33 manual working-class families with young children in a small mining town in Derbyshire. He found no shortage of stimulation at home: the children had plenty of toys, almost all families had pencils, crayons and some children's books; the children were read to and told stories; there was a lot of conversation in the family, and the children were accustomed to meeting a fair number of adults. However, by the age of four the children tended to spend much of their time playing outside rather than in interaction with their parents. These findings suggest that the cruder notions of environmental deficit are mistaken, at least for certain working-class communities. Hubbard himself was most struck by the failure of these working-class parents to see their role as an educational one. Their main concern appeared to be that the child should be healthy, well-fed, well-dressed and happy. More than 80 per cent of the mothers believed that expectations of their children's school performance must largely be based on family endowment of ability. Over 94 per cent believed 'the school would bring it out if anything was there'. Most of the parents feared that any form of helping the child to think and learn might be contrary to school practice.

On the basis of his study, Hubbard is convinced that an attempt should be made to influence working-class attitudes to parenthood. He has tried two main approaches: child development programmes for children in their last year in secondary school and parent classes in infant-welfare clinics. The fifteen-year-old children were encouraged to work with five-year-olds in the infant school; they often showed considerable talent in drawing the children out. Videotapes of their sessions were shown to the infant school teachers, who were sometimes surprised at the verbal fluency of five-year-olds who had been mute in class. Mr Hubbard hopes that from this experience the adolescents will acquire an understanding of how to prepare their own children for school.

For parents, Hubbard has chosen to set up weekly discussions and classes at an Infant Welfare Clinic, rather than use Home Visitors. He thinks that mothers often resent someone coming into their home and implicitly criticizing them, and that it is easier to influence them on the neutral ground of the clinic. These classes should start very early, whilst the child is still an infant. At this time the mother can be made conscious of her importance in helping language development, shown the importance of questioning the child, and answering his questions, of playing with him, reading to him, and discussing with him what has been read. She can be shown how to devise play material from household possessions, and how to help the child to use it creatively. In this group situation the mothers can share ideas and discuss their problems, and work towards the reality of his aim, 'every home a nursery school'. Mr Hubbard has devised a series of videotapes which have proved useful in such classes. He plans to evaluate the effectiveness of the groups by using questionnaire and interviews with the mothers at the end of the project.

In contrast, John Nicholls and Ethel Seaman at Norwich argue that parent education is best assisted by using 'Education Visitors' to help the parents become aware of the child's intellectual needs. An analogy is drawn with Health Visitors—just as trained nurses help the mother to see the child's health needs, trained teachers are needed to help her assist his intellectual development. The scheme differs in two important respects from most 'Home Visiting' schemes; firstly the Education Visitors work with the mother and not the child, and secondly, instead of working to a prescribed programme, showing the mother how to use toys, etc., their brief is the more open-ended one of helping the mother to see the educational opportunities of the home.

These differences derive from the underlying rationale of the scheme, that the young child's language development depends on the quality of the family interactions. For this reason they argue that only limited benefit could come from working directly with the child, whilst prescribing to the mother exactly what she should do is likely to undermine her confidence. Instead the Education Visitors should support the parents; discussions about the child's development and his daily routine will often alert the parents to aspects of his needs which they had not previously considered. A third unusual feature of the scheme is the insistence that the Education Visitors should be trained and experienced teachers. There are two main reasons for this: just as the Health Visitor is respected by the parents for her expertise, so they argue that the Education Visitor needs to be an acknowledged expert in her field. Secondly, after a two year term of duty it is planned that the Visitor should return to teaching, and it is felt that both the teacher and the school system would be greatly enriched by the greater understanding gained of families and their interactions with schools, and of the complexities of early language development.

In the first stage of the study ten teachers, after an initial training, were each attached to a family, selected on the basis that it included a baby of one, and an older child who was under-achieving at school because of deficiencies in language usage. No immigrants were included. The teachers, who were volunteers, working in their spare time and at their own expense, visited the families once a month, and met frequently for discussion amongst themselves. During this period it was felt that a substantial change in parental attitudes occurred. Norwich Education Authority has now appointed one full-time paid Education Visitor, who will be seconded from teaching for two years. She will visit all parents within a given district with a child aged one, until such time as the child enters nursery school or playgroup. It is considered important not to offer a service for 'deprived' children, but one available to all families in the community. Volunteer visitors are also continuing their work.

Yet another approach to parent education is that of Eric Midwinter and the 'Home Link' experiment in Liverpool. The aim of the venture is to train and use working-class mothers as home visitors. The project is located on a new housing estate, Netherley, where experimental and control areas have been designated. One hundred parents with children under five were located through the records of the general practitioner and their attitudes to pre-school development assessed by test. Twelve of the mothers were invited to train as home visitors, and a ten-week training course is planned for them. The mothers will work as volunteers, backed by the resources of a toy lending library. The underlying rationale of the study is that the mothers need to be helped to see theia importrnce as educators of their own children, and that it is better to use the resources of the community, i.e. other mothers, than to depend extensively on professional expertise. The training course will be geared to emphasizing the importance of the mother spending time playing with and talking to the child.

Margaret Clark of Strathclyde University is involved in a parent education study with Bill Donachy in Renfrewshire. In this study Health Visitors are being used to give guidance to parents of pre-school children about the best ways of using books and toys with their children. One group of parents has a child at nursery school, and the other has not. A third group of parents is attending classes, mostly run by teachers, at their nearest primary school, whilst school aides look after their children. The assessment measures used include interview and attitude scales with parents, and developmental tests with children. Improvements seem to occur in the children's test scores, but Margaret Clark sees the main benefit in terms of changes in parental attitudes to school, and changes in teachers' attitudes to parents. She believes that these kind of changes are not likely to follow from attendance at pre-school, but may be more crucial for the child's continuing development than any immediate test gains in the early years.

It will be noted that there is no built-in evaluation in most of these parent education programmes, mainly because of inadequate funding. At least three changes are assumed to occur as a result of parent education: a change in expressed parental attitudes to child rearing and school, a change in parent behaviour, and a change in the children's achievements. Whilst changes in the first or the third variable (as assessed by standardized tests) or both have been recorded in some studies, changes in parent behaviour are only inferred. American experience suggests that just as the effect of school programmes for the young child 'wash-out' without later reinforcement, so the improvements in children's test scores which may accompany home visiting schemes are not sustained once the visiting stops.

It is not known whether changes in parental attitudes 'wash-out' too, nor whether changes in parental behaviour ever in fact occurred. The improvement in the child's test scores may reflect a greater ease in the question and answer situation; that is, it may result from the home visitor's interactions with the children, rather than from any change in parent behaviour. Alternatively, if parent behaviour did change, but such changes were reversed when home visiting stopped, it may be that the parent was taught behaviour specific to a particular age range of children, e.g. to play with the child with toys, advice which would offer little guidance once the child prefers to play with his age-mates, or it may be that without reinforcement the kind of parent–child relationship which is customary in the local community re-asserts itself.

However, much of the thinking about parent education seems both psychologically and sociologically simplistic. We are coming increasingly to understand that what the child learns, and how he learns it, depends to an extent on the characteristics of the communication system within the family. Bernstein has pointed out that this system is related to the distribution of power within the family, and within the wider society. What kind of knowledge seems to a mother important to communicate to her child, and how she communicates it, is probably affected by many complex factors, which include her own position in society and her expectations and understanding of what her children need. Many of the factors are very objective, e.g. whilst educational success is essential for middle-class children if they are to retain the same position in society as their parents, this motivation does not exist for working-class parents. Working-class mothers have fewer resources, in terms of leisure and space, with which to entertain their children, and for these reasons are more likely to encourage them to 'play out'. The incidence of mild depression in working-class mothers with young children is known to be very high, much higher than amongst middle-class mothers with children of the same age (Brown, 1975). This is an additional factor which is likely to affect communication within the family, and from this point of view, changes in the mother's life may be more effective in altering her communication with her children than encouragement to play with them or read to them.

8. The learning environment of the home

Because of the essentially private nature of family life we know very little about how learning occurs at home. By the age of three there are well marked social class differences in children's behaviour, certainly with respect to both language development and usage (c.f. Joan Tough) and play interests (c.f. Tizard and Philps). However, we know very little about the crucial aspects of the environment concerned, or of the different teaching strategies responsible. Most theories have little empirical basis, and depend either on extrapolation from observations of mothers' behaviour in highly artificial situations (e.g. the famous Hess and Shipman study) or on inferences from the child's behaviour, which are not confirmed in any systematic study (e.g. early theories that working-class children received inadequate verbal stimulation). Conversely, we know very little about the effect on development of environmental variation, e.g. the extent to which perceptual-motor skills depend on various kind of play experiences.

(i) *General environmental studies of homes*

An important sector of British research is currently concerned with these problems. Charmian Davie, at Keele, is investigating a simple but basic question: How do young children who do not attend preschool spend their day? How much time do they spend in adult company how much in playing on their own, or with siblings or peers? How much time does the mother or father spend interacting with the child? How much, and how varied, is the play equipment available to him?

Brian Jackson of the National Childminding Research and Development Unit is making two descriptive studies of young children at home. In the first, he is studying six four-year-old children living in a medium-sized industrial town. All will go to the same primary school. One is a child from a family that has lived in Yorkshire for as long as they know, one has West Indian parents, another, Italian, and another has Pakistani parents. Alongside these Huddersfield-born children are a Chinese-born boy from the local take-away shop, and a suddenly arrived Ugandan refugee born in Kampala. The research involves asking few questions but rather living with the families and observing and recording their different cultural expressions of emotional, social and mental life. The food, toys, play, motivation, relationships and rituals are observed. As the children grow, the research monitors the apparent effect in the home of the media, of early literacy; outside the home, of friends and contacts—and finally the crucial entry to the school. Along the way, the position continually explored, and when possible tested, is how far and in what way the cultural inheritance of a normal young child in a thriving city is ignored, dismissed or celebrated.

A second study is concerned with Chinese children in Britain. Their numbers appear to have grown very considerably over the last decade, largely owing to the rise of the take-away food trade, and to the retention of British passport rights in Hong Kong. Teachers seem to have very seldom penetrated their homes, to be unaware of their language or culture, and to believe them to be only temporary migrants. A study of the families, though, suggests that they are permanently settled, that the number of young children concerned is increasing, and that what teachers see as oriental impassiveness in the children is often bewilderment and depression at being isolated in an alien environment.

(ii) Studies of language in the home

Since Bernstein's early formulations, many investigators have seen the language of the family and the meanings conveyed as the most important medium by which social class differences in cognition are affected. However, until very recently there has been little direct evidence of verbal communication in the home. A valuable source of information about conversational exchange within families is now available in a series of tape-recordings made by Anthony Wootton in Aberdeen (Wootton, 1974). Three four-hour recordings were made during the course of a week in the homes of each of 20 young children, using radio microphones. Half were children of semi-skilled workers, and half were the children of professional workers, managers, or business proprietors.

Analysis of the data revealed that middle-class children spoke more often to their parents than did working-class children, that the discussions which they had with them tended to be longer, and that a greater proportion of their talk to parents was in the context of play. Middle-class parents tended to question their children more often than working-class parents, and to make comments which had the effect of extending the dialogue sequences, transmitting information, and encouraging the child to think in terms of validity, causality, and conceptual hierarchies. In contrast, the working-class parents tended to ask few questions, and to respond in a minimal way to questions and comments made by the child. The same trend was apparent in fantasy play; middle-class, but not working-class, parents tended to use the opportunity provided by the play to extend the child's information and thinking strategies.

Perhaps because more opportunity was offered them, middle-class children asked more dialogue-dependent questions than did working-class children, although there was little difference in the overall social class incidence of 'Why' questions. Wootton argues that the evidence indicates that the working-class child is left more in charge of his own construction of reality than is the middle-class child, and that his understanding of the world is not so closely articulated with his parents' meanings. He relates this to social class differences in the parent–child relationship, and especially to the parents' conception of the guiding role they should take with their children.

The numbers in this study are small, but because of the length of each recording the data could form a valuable source of hypotheses. We cannot, of course, from this study draw any inference about the relationship between maternal teaching strategies and the children's linguistic ability as assessed by tests or in any contrived situation, since only spontaneous conversation at home is available.

This lack will to some extent be rectified in an ongoing study by Gordon Wells in Bristol, although since his speech samples last for only 90 seconds the rich interactional sequences collected by Wootton will not be available. Two groups of 64 children aged 15 and 39 months at the time of the study are involved. Each child will be studied for $2\frac{1}{4}$ years, so that data will be collected for a total age range of $1\frac{1}{4}$–$5\frac{1}{2}$ years. The child's spontaneous speech in the home is sampled at three-monthly intervals by the use of radio transmitters attached to the child's clothing. Twenty-four ninety-second samples of the child's speech at different periods in the day are recorded, and on the same evening the tape is replayed to the mother in order to get contextual information on the samples.

The model of analysis (Wells, 1974) seeks to relate the meaning intentions of each child utterance both to the surface structure through which these are realized and to the conversational context in which they occur. Initial computer analysis of the coded data will seek to establish development patterns in individuals with respect to the major categories in the theoretical model. Comparisons will then be made across children in terms of sex and social class, and in terms of information obtained in an interview with the mother when the child is $3\frac{1}{2}$ about family attitudes and practices with regard to linguistic acquisition.

Every three months, besides recording the child's spontaneous speech, he is given specially developed linguistic tests, aimed to assess his ability to comprehend and imitate a range of sentence types and spatial and temporal relational terms. From this data, as well as IQ scores and other information, it is hoped to answer the following questions:

(1) To what extent is the sequence of linguistic development invariant across children?

(2) What is the relation between a child's spontaneous verbal behaviour and his linguistic ability as assessed by tests of comprehension and production?

(3) How great is the variation between children of the same age with respect to

(a) their level of linguistic ability? (b) their habitual use of language both as speaker and as hearer?

(4) To what extent can the variations in (3) be attributed to

(a) differences in physical development and/or measured intelligence?

(b) sex, position in family, socioeconomic status of the family, etc.?

(c) specific cognitive and linguistic characteristics of their experience, such as the contexts in which speech is used, the frequency of model structures in parental speech, etc.?

Basil Bernstein and his associates at London Institute of Education are currently carrying out a study concerned with the interaction between social class and the structure of transmission and acquisition of educationally relevant procedures and performances. The structure of transmission will initially be analysed in terms of the classification and framing procedures of families (Bernstein, 1971; 1974). A small number of families, children and educational contexts will be studied, using naturalistic, experimental and interview methods.

The focus of the research will be the criteria, implicit or explicit, used in the process of transmission. The criteria used by the transmitter will be studied in regulative, instructional, interpersonal and imaginative contexts. Bernstein considers these four contexts as eliciting different *language functions*; for it is very possible that an inter-actional sequence may range across more than one context. He asks the following questions:

(1) If language functions are regarded as options, which options or combinations does the transmitter select in which inter-actional sequences?
(2) What is the relationship between differences in the structure of transmission, the language functions selected *and* the form of their realization?

The criteria, implicitly or explicitly realized by the transmitter which he hopes to study, are the following:

(1) Focusing criteria: *this* is more important to attend to than *that*.
(2) Evaluative criteria: this performance is better than that.
(3) Recognition criteria: this sign is better than that, as an indication that the performance has been effectively acquired.
(4) Pedagogic criteria: these practices rather than those are more effective media for acquisition of performances.
(5) Developmental criteria: the principles which relate activities dis-chronically and synchronically.

He expects that the developmental criteria will determine pedagogic criteria which in turn will act selectively upon focusing evaluative and recognition criteria. The above formulation draws attention to the highly selective nature of transmission and so points to the values/ideology upon which it is based. The process of acquisition is equally selective—what is acquired may be more or less similar to or different from what is transmitted—but it is constrained by the structure of transmission. The school may operate with similar or different focusing, evaluative, recognition, pedagogic and developmental criteria.

In general, Bernstein argues that we have good reason for believing that social class regulates the distribution of the dominant meanings transmitted, the form of their realization and the context of their acquisition. However, he expects that as the classification and framing procedures of the family and school varies so will the structure of transmission, the language function selected and the form of their realization, the criteria which regulate learning, the sociolinguistic codings of the children and the field of cognitive relevance. A major focus of the research will be upon a detailed study of the *processes* underlying differences in transmission and acquisition *within* and between social classes. The major research endeavour will be to work out methods for the study of such processes.

One major longitudinal study has been concerned to relate aspects of early mother–child interaction to later child achievement. Blurton-Jones and his associates at the Institute of Child Health, London, are currently carrying out a short-term longitudinal study of 60 middle-class first-born children. Its main aims are to trace the course of attachment behaviour, to examine the relationship between different kinds of attachment behaviour, and to relate the child's attachment behaviour to various aspects of maternal behaviour. The development of language, and of aggressive behaviour, and the relation of both of these to aspects of maternal behaviour are also an important part of the study.

The children have been observed at 15, 21, and 27 months, and it is planned to see them again at 33 and 39 months. At each age the children are observed on five occasions. They are brought on three occasions to a playroom in the Institute, with three other children in the study, all the mothers and any younger sibs. On a fourth occasion they are observed without other children in this playroom with their mothers, both alone with her and whilst she is being interviewed. The fifth observation period is in the child's own home. In addition to recording the social behaviour of the child on these occasions, and the mother's behaviour towards the child, several contrived separation situations are observed. Also, at each age the children are observed in the park with their mothers, in order to record the relative roles of mother and child in maintaining proximity. Later it is planned to observe each child's peer interactions in nursery school. At each age the children are tested with the Reynell Development Language Scale, and their scores related to various measures of mother–child interaction.

The study is only halfway through and not many results are yet available. Some leads that seem to have emerged are that the children's

expressive language development is related not to proximity maintenance, but to the speed with which the mother responds to his
conversational overtures, and that there appears to be a relationship
between the frequency of a child's unprovoked attacks on older
children and the manner in which his mother responds to his crying. It
is planned to assess the language development and educational attainments of these children at five and at seven, in order to see whether
these can be related to aspects of early mother–child interaction. It is also
planned to make a short longitudinal study of mother–child interactions
in working-class families. The emphasis of this study would be more
on the relationship between early mother–child interactions and later
language and educational attainments, and less on the development of
attachment behaviour *sui generis*. Thus low maternal responsiveness in
vocal and other 'distance attachment' interactions is expected to
predict low performance on language and school attainments, and low
responsiveness to physical contact and crying to predict a tendency to
unprovoked aggressive behaviour to peers.

The relationship between language retardation, behaviour problems
and some aspects of the environment has been studied by Naomi
Richman and Jim Stevenson of the Hospital for Sick Children, London.
A one-in-four random sample of families with three-year-olds living
in an outer London suburb were interviewed. Of the 800 three year
olds, 15 per cent were judged to show mild behaviour problems, and
7 per cent moderate to severe problems. There were no significant
differences in the prevalence of problems by sex, social class, or
whether the parents were immigrants. The data on language development is not fully analysed, but on a provisional estimate 3–5 per cent
of the three-year-olds had delayed language development, that is,
were not speaking in phrases of three or more words. The factors
associated with delayed language development appeared to be the
presence of behaviour problems in the child, over-crowding in the
home, and a large number of sibs.

9. Mother–child interactions in infancy

An important sector of current British research in the field of early
childhood development is concerned with infant behaviour. This area
seems at first sight remote from problems of pre-school education, but
as we shall see the ideas which are being worked out have important
educational implications. There are marked similarities of approach,
as well as characteristic differences, in the research which is being

carried out in different centres. In all the centres no sharp distinction is made between cognitive and social processes. On the contrary, cognitive skills are seen as being shaped by social interaction, and are studied only within the context of social interaction. Secondly, all centres emphasize the role which the infant plays in determining his own experience. It is argued that from birth the child has an individuality which determines how he responds to parental treatment and even to an extent determines the nature of this treatment. This is another reason for studying, not the infant on his own, but the interactions that occur between the infant and his mother, and the way in which each adapts his behaviour to that of the other. This common approach results in methodological similarities—because the subject of interest is the study of interactions, data analysis is concerned with the timing and sequence of behaviour. For this purpose the rather gross observational measures used in the past have proved inadequate, and most centres rely a good deal on frame-by-frame analysis of films and videotapes.

Rudolf Schaffer and his colleagues at Strathclyde University have explored the characteristics of mother–infant vocal interactions. They have been struck by the turn-taking nature of mother's and baby's vocalizations. The two rarely vocalize at the same time and the alternation so produced is thus somewhat like a conversation between adults. This turn-taking Schaffer believes is probably due to the mother's sensitivity. The baby, in other words, emits bursts of vocalization, and it is left to the mother to fill in the pause. What one then observes is a synchronization of the two sets of responses which in fact does not yet reflect a true social reciprocity but is entirely due to the mother letting herself be paced by the infant's periodic behaviour. This conclusion is also suggested by findings from another of his ongoing studies, in which he is examining the visual synchrony of mother and baby in a strange environment containing a number of large, prominently placed toys. The baby looks at the various toys in turn and the mother, taking her cue from his behaviour and usually responding with a very fine sense of timing, also looks at them. Thus the couple share by such visual means an interest in some feature of the environment that is in fact entirely determined by the baby. This is also an example of an interaction situation that shows all the hallmarks of interpersonal synchrony; again, however, it is a one-way affair, for right up to the end of the first year one rarely sees the infant visually following the mother's looking behaviour. Hence Schaffer suspects that the key aspect of maternal behaviour in assisting development is its contingency, that is, what the mother does to help the child is not so much to provide him with stimulation, but to respond appropriately and at the right interval of time to his signals.

John and Elizabeth Newson at Nottingham work from a very similar viewpoint. They argue that most of what the infant learns is learned in the context of social interaction. The mother responds to the signals the baby emits, and it is this contingent re-activity of the mother which makes her an object of compelling interest to the baby. The non-verbal communication thus established is an essential prerequisite to the development of verbal communication. The Newsons argue that the quality of the child's language development depends on the degree of successful communication it has had with an adult since birth. This process, by which mother–infant communication is initiated and sustained forms the subject for a number of research projects going on in their unit; these include a study of the communicative significance of reaching behaviour in infants, a study of imitative behaviour in infants and their mothers, and studies of communication sequences between mongol and deaf babies and their mothers. In all the projects periodic observations of mother–infant pairs are arranged in semi-standardized situations. Frame-by-frame analysis of videotape sequences forms an essential part of their approach.

Martin Richards' study of infant behaviour is linked to a longitudinal study. He and his associates in Cambridge are studying 100 mothers and their first- or second-born children from birth to five years of age. Martin Richards and Judy Bernal have particularly directed their research towards a detailed observational study of mother–infant interactions. Like other workers in this area, they have made use of frame-by-frame analysis of films to study the timing and sequence of such interactions as an exchange of smiles. They have also tried to trace the influence of newborn characteristics on the pattern of interaction during the first year—for example, upon feeding, sleeping and crying patterns. Another interest is the influence of obstetric medication on mother–infant interaction.

As well as looking at longitudinal relationships, two cross-sectional studies are being carried out. Frances Barnes is studying these same children at $2\frac{1}{2}$–3 years, and her interest is mainly in analysing the patterns of communication in the family in as far as it is informative about the underlying relationships—the ideas here derive ultimately from Bateson's studies. Data are largely obtained through observation and the analysis of tape recordings. The same sample of children is being studied again at four and five years by Paul Light, who is working in more structured testing situations with the children. The two main emphases are a battery of Piaget-derived measures of cognitive development and a battery of tests designed to evaluate the child's ability to perceive the perceptions of other people, to 'see the other person's point of view' (the ideas here derive from G. Mead).

Martin Richards' and Judy Bernal's studies of the first year of life suggest that the nature of the mother–child interaction depends as much on the qualities of the child as the mother. Some babies from the start sleep badly or seem difficult to manage, and these difficulties seem to occur irrespective of how the mother tries to deal with them. They may have been caused initially by physiological events in pregnancy or childbirth, associated perhaps with a temporary diminution of blood supply to the foetus. Richards argues that even if changes in behaviour related to birth events only last a few days, they could have very long-term effects if they modify the mother–child interaction. Infants with less favourable birth records are 'difficult' babies, and feeds go less smoothly. Particular styles of parental interaction may be set up at this time in response to the infant's behaviour. Later differences seen in the children may well be the outcome of both the continuing effects of the infant's central nervous system status and of the cumulative result of the altered parental interactions. Development is a highly complex interactive process and in Richards' view it is too simplistic to talk of either infant or parent effects. One is always dealing with both. On the basis of his work, Richards argues that the socio-psychological approach to early development is one-sided. If birth events do have long-term effects there is much that could be done to improve matters. Comprehensive health care programmes are very effective in reducing perinatal mortality (Baird and Thompson, 1969), but they might also alleviate many of the developmental problems that are the targets for the educational early-intervention programmes. None of this means that these latter programmes are necessarily ineffective or that they should be stopped, simply that they represent a one-sided approach to a developmental and social problem. As yet, we hardly know how to design and mount a post-natal early-intervention programme, but we do know how to improve obstetric care, and programmes in the field are relatively cheap.

Jerome Bruner and his associates in Oxford are also centring their research around mother–infant pairs in the first year of life. Bruner and Macfarlane are exploring two possible factors that operate to put an infant and mother at risk of failing to develop a maturing interaction, namely, severe ante-natal maternal anxiety and prolonged separation during the neo-natal period. Mother–infant pairs who have undergone more than ten days of separation after delivery, owing to the pre-maturity of the baby, will be contrasted with 'normal' matching pairs. They will be observed in hospital, and when the infant is four months and twelve months old. The alertness, irritability and activity level of the infant will be measured, as well as the mother's sensitivity to the infant, and the extent to which she notices and responds to the baby's actions and needs.

A second study directed by Bruner is concerned with the transition from pre-linguistic to linguistic communication. Up to now, studies of language acquisition have been based on samples of the earliest speech. However, Bruner argues that before the child utters his first words he has acquired certain fundamental concepts for regulating joint action and directing his attention jointly with an adult caretaker. The communication which goes on between child and adult before language develops depends on the implicit possession by the child of such concepts as agent, action, object and location, as well as the notion of a jointly attended topic on which comments can be made. The transition to speech involves the working out of routines between caretaker and infant whereby linguistic forms are combined with episodes involving action and attention, and become used for regulating signals. It is not surprising, then, that when two- and three-word utterances appear, they take the form of agent-object, action-recipient of action, etc., since language develops in the context of shared action and attention.

Bruner proposes to trace the child's acquisition of certain key 'proto-semantic' conceptual schemes, and then to examine the manner in which language is combined with these to extend and elaborate them. Mother–infant pairs will be observed fortnightly from the time when the infant is six months of age until he is producing two- or three-word utterances. Videotape recordings will be made. Because of his belief that both prelinguistic and linguistic communication develop in the course of mutually regulating activity and attention, some structure will be imposed on the observation sessions. The mothers will be asked to draw their child's attention to something, to allow their child to enlist their attention, to feed, bath and play with the child, and induce him to carry out a task. The babies will also be given certain formal concept tests.

OTHER RESEARCH TOPICS

10. Cognitive skills of young children

Pre-school education should have as its foundation an understanding of the growth of intellect in the first years of life. The main contributor to this field has of course been Piaget, but in fact he seems to have had very little impact on nursery school practice. Piagetian theory is at times used as a rationale for learning through play, but it was probably Dewey rather than Piaget who was the main theoretical influence on pre-school education.

Peter Bryant, at Oxford, argues that in fact Piaget usually takes the environment as given, hence cognitive development tends to be seen as an inevitable process which hardly needs assistance by teachers. Moreover, because much of Piaget's experimental work has been concerned with showing what children *can't* do at certain stages in their development, teachers' have drawn from this the inference that children's intellects are very limited, and that there is little that they can be taught in the early years. However, just as there has been a recent emphasis on the fact that the language a person uses, and the way he uses it, depends very much on the particular setting, so a re-evaluation of Piaget has suggested that his conclusions derive very much from the specific situations he set up. Bryant argues that in certain situations young children are capable of considerable intellectual feats, which may be unsuspected by parents and teachers. (The same point has, of course, been made by Bruner and other psychologists working with infants.) Much of his work has been concerned with re-evaluating Piaget's hypotheses from this point of view (Bryant, 1974).

One recent study, for example, was concerned with transitive inferences. Piaget's experiment involves showing the child two sticks A and B of different lengths, and asking him which is the longer, and then asking him to make the same judgement about sticks C and D. He is then asked whether A is longer than C. According to Piaget, children cannot make the necessary transitive inference until the age of seven or eight. Educationalists have concluded from this that certain mathematical operations, e.g. measurement, should not be taught until this age. However, Bryant has shown that even four-year-old children are very well able to make a transitive inference provided that they can remember the relationships on which the inference is based at the time that they have to make it. Poor recall should not be confused with inability to reason. Bryant also shows that conservation occurs in four-year-old children. In the past, psychologists have tested for conservation in situations in which there was a conflict between the immediate evidence of the child's senses and the application of the principle of conservation. If, however, the experimental situation does not involve such a conflict it becomes apparent that most four-year-olds understand conservation. He concludes that young children have considerable intellectual ability and should be encouraged to use it. When considering curriculum development it is more important to recognize the competence of children, and to find ways of using their abilities, rather than to emphasize the operations which they are not capable of doing.

Margaret Donaldson in Edinburgh has also been led by her experimental work to conclude that in some ways Piaget's views of cognitive development are seriously wrong. In particular, she too believes that Piaget has underestimated the inferential skills of young children. This is because of her conviction that the normal growth of reasoning cannot be effectively studied in isolation from considerations of how children interpret language—and in particular how they interpret what experimenters say to them in formal test situations. This conviction has led her to a series of researches concerned with the comprehension of comparatives and quantifiers—terms such as more, less, same, different, all, some, none—these having been chosen for study because of their central role in tasks that have been used to investigate the growth of deductive inference, that is, tasks concerned with conservation, class inclusion and so on (Donaldson, 1970, 1972; Donaldson and Balfour, 1968; Donaldson and Lloyd, in press; Donaldson and McGarrigle, in press).

One example of the results is as follows. The children (age range three to five) were shown two display shelves. On one of these there was a row of four cars, on the other a row of five, the cars being arranged so that there were four pairs in one-to-one correspondence while the 'odd man out' projected at one end. When the children were asked: 'Are there more cars here or more cars here?' they generally answered correctly.

The experimenter then enclosed each row of cars in a joined set of garages. The crucial feature of this changed situation was that the four cars were enclosed in a set of four garages, which was thus full, where-as the five cars were enclosed in a set of six garages, so that one garage was empty. When the question was repeated a substantial number of the children changed their judgement and decided that there were now more cars in the row containing four than in the row containing five. The children's comments suggested strongly that it was the impression of 'fullness' which determined this change; and results from other studies confirmed the belief that the attribute of fullness was powerfully salient for children in this age-group.

What we have to account for, Donaldson argues, is the fact that the shifts in interpretation are related in highly systematic ways to the contexts in which the language is uttered. If they were random we might simply say that the child lacked a precise understanding of the meaning and leave the matter there. Since they are not random, then, if the lexicon is undifferentiated, rules of some kind must be constraining the children's judgements. The explanation which Donaldson proposes is that there are rules of non-linguistic kinds interacting with the lexical (and indeed also with the syntactic) rules to determine how language is to be interpreted. The general notion is that the linguistic rules specify the area within which the final interpretation will lie— for instance, the child knows that 'more' refers to a difference in magnitude and not, say, to colour. But the precise interpretation which the utterance finally receives depends on the interaction of the linguistic rules with others of a non-linguistic kind that have to do with salience (perceptual or conceptual) and with the weight which is to be attached to particular features of the context in which the utterance is heard. Donaldson suggests the term 'local rules' for these non-linguistic determinants, since they have to do with circumstances locally obtaining and specify a kind of 'local meaning' for the language. She believes that recognition of their mode of operation forces on us a reconsideration of much that has been asserted in recent years both about the growth of reasoning and about the acquisition of language.

Like Bryant, Margaret Donaldson, on the basis of her work, queries the adequacy of the current nursery school faith that the child will learn what is needed without explicit teaching. She believes that the child's skill at drawing inferences could be considerably developed by the appropriate teaching strategies, in which he was involved in dialogue with an adult who had this aim to the fore. Another study at the interface between language and cognition is Maureen Shields' analysis of speech samples of 153 children aged three-to-five-years (Institute of Education, London). The samples were collected in 10 pre-school centres, with the aim of recording in a variety of situations the language forms available to young children and the developmental sequence they exhibit. In addition, through an analysis of the context setting of the language Maureen Shields hopes to reach an understanding of the cognitive and social function of the language for the child. An immediate educational 'pay-off' came from an analysis of which contexts and communication situations elicited the most fluent and complex speech from the child.

Shields' analysis of the ways in which language becomes more complex and varied during these years is not yet complete. Her evidence suggests that language development is connected with cognitive development, e.g. the increase which occurs in the use of stative verbs of cognition, perception and feeling she believes is probably linked to the development of self-awareness, while the increase in the use of modal and quasi-modal auxiliaries she argues is related to an increasing grasp of certainties/uncertainties, possibilities, probabilities, necessities and degree of obligation. Shields found very marked interpersonal and material contextual effects on children's language production. In any situation, domination by the adult tended to reduce the linguistic output of children; the play situations which favoured longer and more complex utterances were imaginative play with model worlds and socio-dramatic play with role taking.

11. Provision and evaluation of services for the under-fives

At the beginning of this review it was pointed out that many women for a variety of reasons no longer wish to undertake full-time care of their young children. The government, however, recognizes no statutory responsibility to provide education or care for children until they are five, and the number of day nursery and nursery school places available has until recently been very limited. Consequently a wide variety of informal arrangements have grown up. Large numbers of children are cared for by childminders or private nurseries. Parents have organized their own playgroups, and local authorities and voluntary bodies have organized playgroups for children in special need. There is very little knowledge of how extensive these arrangements are, or of the characteristics of families who use the various services. How many young children go to playgroups or childminders? How adequately do existing services cater for the needs of families with young children? What new services, or alterations to existing services, are needed? What effect will the proposed expansion of nursery education have on the existing services, and how far will it meet unmet needs?

A number of people argue that the decision to expand nursery education appears to have been made more because of its supposed efficacy in preventing later school failure than in response to the needs of young children or their families. A half-day school session does little to meet the needs of even part-time working mothers, whilst children from families with a great many problems are unlikely to be sent to nursery school. Such families need extra help in the form of a collection service for the children, and other forms of help for the mothers. On the other hand, many people express concern lest the expansion of nursery schools should lead to the collapse of the play-group movement, and the consequent loss to the mother's own development and to that of the community of the benefit of parental involvement in the education of her own child.

The National Children's Bureau has recently carried out three studies of pre-school services. Anne Joseph described the characteristics of playgroups in an area of high social need; Dorothy Birchall attempted on behalf of a local authority to assess the needs of families within that locality for day-care provision for under-fives. Sandhya Naidoo monitored a nursery centre which provided day care for normal, physically handicapped and socially handicapped children. Her concern was with the organizational viability of the undertaking, its staffing needs, and the problems it met.

The Bureau has now funds available for two further research projects concerned with pre-school children. The first will survey pre-school playgroups which have been set up for children in high need. They will try to describe the various criteria of high need used by the organizing bodies, and the extent to which the parents for whom the facilities are provided in fact take advantage of them. The second project will be concerned with nursery centres, that is, pre-school centres which combine education and long day care. The investigators will study the practical problems of setting-up and running such institutions, and attempt to assess their impact on the families using them, and on the local community. They will also assess the development of the children attending the centre using a new developmental chart which is currently undergoing field test trials. This chart has been devised so that it can be used by nursery staff. It is intended to have the dual function of sensitizing the staff to a wide range of the children's activities, and providing a profile of the child's development.

A major survey, 'Child Health and Education in the Seventies' directed by Neville Butler, from Bristol, is being made of all children born in the week 5th–11th April, 1970, who are now living in Great Britain. The main aims of the survey are: (a) To examine the development of children identified in the perinatal period as being at risk, because of adverse birth or obstetric factors, and (b) to document the utilization of child health, care and educational facilities by all the families in the survey in the first five years of life. In addition, all known pre-school institutions in Great Britain (nursery schools, nursery classes, playgroups, day nurseries and private nurseries) are being sent a postal questionnaire, in order to obtain information on such matters as staffing, parental involvement, hours of opening, allocation of places, facilities available, and daily routine.

Joyce Watt at Aberdeen is currently engaged in a fact-finding survey of all existing pre-school provisions in Fife, as well as an analysis of the attitudes of parents toward present and proposed provision, with particular reference to their own role within it, and a survey of the attitudes of professionals from each service towards their individual and complementary educational roles. She points out that we don't have enough information about the characteristics of families who use different kinds of provision—Do those most in need get the most help? At a later stage she hopes to organize pilot projects concerned to promote collaboration between the various authorities and professions concerned with the pre-school child. The methods used might include regular discussions between representatives of the authorities, joint lectures and discussions for students on various courses, a collaborative nursery school/playgroup scheme and collaborative assistance of families in need by, e.g. a teacher and a social worker. What she is working towards is a method by which the professional expertise of the teacher, social worker and health visitor can be harnessed to the grassroots enthusiasm of the playgroup movement. 'Action research' is needed which would look at this collaborative process in action. In addition, the educational contribution of the health visitor needs further investigation. For families who do not use playgroups or schools, she could play an important role, e.g. she could make useful liaisons between such families, and encourage informal contacts.

Willem van der Eyken recently carried out a study from Brunel

University aimed to identify the characteristics of families who did, and did not, make use of playgroup facilities. The area chosen was a fairly prosperous working-class estate in Hillingdon. A survey showed that 87 families on the estate had children aged three and four. All of these mothers were interviewed, using a 180-item schedule, which included questions about the parents' occupation, income, social contacts, educational background, attitude to school, etc.; all were asked if they would like their children to attend a playgroup, and their reasons for wanting or not wanting a playgroup. They were also given the Rotter scale, which attempts to measure feelings of alienation and helplessness. Two-thirds of the families said they would use a playgroup if it were provided. Some months later the local authority put a playgroup into the Estate, to be run by the Tenant's Association, and the families were notified verbally that the playgroup was due to start. Because of the local authority delay some of the children had started primary school.

Of the 77 families left with children aged three and four, 22 mothers (Group 1) did not use the playgroup, 37 mothers (Group 2) sent their children to the playgroup, and 10 mothers (Group 3) were using other pre-school facilities. Group 3 mothers were mostly working, and many were unsupported mothers. Group 1 mothers appeared to be of two types. Some were women who genuinely enjoyed their children, and thought that they would learn more at home than at a playgroup. The others, however, tended to be younger than the rest of the mothers, to have had their children earlier, not to have planned their families, and to have more children; they tended to be less well educated, to think education is less important for girls than for boys and to disapprove of raising the school leaving age. They did not think it was important for children to be prepared for school or to have the experience of mixing with other children in a playgroup. They did not differ in occupation or income from the other groups, but their responses on the Rotter Scale differed. Van der Eyken characterized these mothers as having an immature relationship with their children. Because they felt alienated from society, and tended to have few contacts with their neighbours and families, they needed their children to give them a role identity and were unable to release them earlier than necessary from the home. On the basis of these findings, Van der Eyken recommends that Home Visitors should be used to supplement playgroups. These visitors would not be accepted if they appeared to be sent by officialdom, in the sense that Health Visitors are. Their sympathy must be with the mother, and they should be prepared to offer her support in any way, not just by preparing play materials and showing her how to use them, but with the aim of strengthening her as a person.

A. H. Halsey and Teresa Smith at Oxford are investigating the effect of the proposed expansion of nursery schools and classes on the existing provision for the under-fives. Three districts with an at present unmet demand for services will be selected, and parents of pre-school children will be interviewed before expansion plans take effect, and a year or so after the opening of new schools and classes. Existing pre-school groups will be observed, and their staff interviewed. The two main questions with which the study will be concerned are the differences between voluntary and statutory groups, and the effects of an increase in statutory provision on the voluntary groups. In particular, Halsey and Smith are interested in the nature and extent of parental involvement in voluntary and statutory groups. They will investigate the kind of group structure which is related to various forms of parental involvement, the division of labour between parents and staff over the planning and content of group activities, the extent to which parents are involved in educational activities, and the distinguishing characteristics of parents who are actively involved in the groups. They also hope to monitor changes in the extent and kind of parental involvement as the statutory provision increases. Another area of study will be the general level of demand for pre-school provision, the criteria by which demand is estimated at the local government level, and the changes in demand brought about by increasing provision. They hope to find out, in addition, how parents respond to inadequate provision, that is, what alternative arrangements, if any, they make for pre-school care if the statutory expansion is inadequate.

Brian Jackson of the National Childminding Research and Development Unit at Cambridge is concerned with investigating and attempting to improve the childminding system. He points out that this is the major pre-school system outside the family, involving the care of children in groups of up to 20, by untrained, mainly illegal, but paid childminders. He estimates that about 300,000 children are in the care of illegal childminders. Often the environment in which they may spend twelve hours a day is grossly inadequate, e.g. the children may have no toys or other objects to play with and may never be taken out. Besides a descriptive survey, Brian Jackson is involved in three different projects concerned with improving the childminding service. In one project, illegal childminders are being offered a five-week training course, largely based on visits to nurseries and nursery schools followed by discussions. The children they mind are meanwhile placed in specially set up playgroups. Free transport is provided, and the minders are being paid to attend the course. A second approach involves home-based training. An Action Officer has been appointed who will teach by example in the childminder's home and lend her toys and equipment from a Toy and Resources Library. The third project involves replicating the New York scheme of recruiting and training day-care mothers.

Jack Tizard (Thomas Coram Research Unit) has a radical approach to the problem of identifying need. He explicitly rejects concepts of 'priority' groups and of 'selective' services, i.e. services provided by local authorities according to *their* views of what parents *ought* to have, and substitutes the concept of providing services on demand. He points out that when children reach the age of five services are not only free but are made compulsory. For younger children the provision of services is patchy, the poorest and most hard pressed sections of the population are least well provided for and have to pay most for anything they do receive. A large proportion of parents wish for day services of various sorts for their children, and as Blackstone has shown, most West European countries make much more provision for day-care and pre-school education than we do. In part the need for services arises from secular trends in the employment of women, including women with young children. Such trends are occurring in all developed countries, and among women of all social classes.

Jack Tizard thinks that we are moving to a period when the provision of pre-school services 'on demand' will be seen as an integral part of the social services. He sees it as an important function of research to explore the manner in which really adequate comprehensive services can be set up and their advantages and shortcomings explored. Demonstration projects provide not only models for policy makers to copy or adapt or reject if they don't like them—but also laboratories for research.

Two London Boroughs have accordingly agreed to set up comprehensive Children's Centres, each of which serve a small catchment area with a total population of about 2,000, including roughly 200 children aged nought to five. Each will provide a comprehensive array of services for all pre-school children and their families who want to use them. It is not of course anticipated that all children will attend the centres full-time. One centre has 70 places and one 50, and it is expected that these places will be used by many more children, most of whom, especially at younger ages, will attend only part-time or occasionally. The Centres are open from 8 or 8.30 to 5.30 or 6. Children can attend the centres for whatever hours the parent wishes. The staff complement includes trained teachers, nursery nurses, assistants and students; this is an attempt to cut across the often rigid divisions between the professions, and the distinction between 'care' and 'education'. The centres include a launderette and a toy library and hopefully will develop other services or functions in response to parents' wishes. There is a medical room in each centre which serves as a child welfare clinic. All families with young children in the catchment area are being interviewed and all children given developmental assessments. Two 'control' areas are being studied.

An important aspect of the centres is that they are intended to serve a local community, rather than children in particular need, since Tizard argues that 'a service for the poor is usually a poor service'. The research, as distinct from service side of the project has five objectives:

(1) Through periodic surveys, to assess the needs of pre-school children and their families in particular localities: these to include the 'experimental' area served by the proposed Centre, and 'control' areas. It is recognized that in each area needs are likely to be to some extent specific to that locality; nonetheless by carrying out parallel surveys in areas outside the area of the demonstration project it should be possible to make estimates of the manner in which needs differ among families in different social circumstances, living in different types of locality.

(2) To explore the problems of introducing and monitoring comprehensive pre-school and family services, available free of charge to all families in a defined area, rather than piecemeal and selective services available only to some families. In doing this the demonstration Centre will help to define service needs through operational research rather than through mere verbal inquiry.

(3) To make a close study of costs, and of administrative and operational problems, of running a comprehensive and locally based service for pre-school children and their families.

(4) To examine the effects of the services provided upon the wellbeing of the families and on the development of the children receiving them.

(5) To evaluate the developmental assessments and to monitor the health and illnesses of children.

12. Research concerned with the education and development of young severely subnormal children

Investigators concerned with the pre-school education of severely retarded and normal children both address themselves to the same range of problems, e.g. the understanding of developmental processes, the relationship between language and other aspects of cognitive development, the provision of services, curriculum development and parent education. However, there are several respects in which educational research with the severely retarded presents special features, and for this reason the projects in this area are grouped separately. Social class in most cases ceases to be an important variable. Parent education assumes a new dimension, since unlike parent education for normal children it becomes a service requested by the parents, because of the serious problems with which their children present them. Hence they are usually highly motivated to change their children's behaviour and if necessary even their own. Further, most research workers are now convinced that severely retarded children learn so slowly by incidental learning that the traditional nursery school curriculum is not appropriate for them, and some more highly structured teaching becomes essential. Finally, most research in this area is explicitly oriented towards assisting parents and teachers: even 'basic' studies are usually undertaken because of their possible implications in terms of an educational programme.

Joanna Ryan at Cambridge has made a longitudinal study of language development in two groups of severely subnormal children living at home, one of whom had Down's syndrome, and compared their development with that of children of average intelligence. The groups were initially matched for Stanford-Binet mental age, (about three years) social class of parents, and sex ratio. Initially, the retarded children were inferior in some, but not all, aspects of language. They were markedly inferior in understanding prepositions and immediate memory for sentences; in spontaneous speech their mean length of utterance was significantly less, and fewer of their utterances contained both a noun phrase and a verb phrase. There was no difference between the groups in naming and recognizing pictures or in the amount of spontaneous speech. The two retarded groups were re-tested after an interval of 14 months, the normal children after $4\frac{1}{2}$ months. During this period there was no development in a number of aspects of the retarded children's language, including mean length of utterance. Joanna Ryan suspects that the retarded child's communication problem results in both teacher and mother talking to him in an over-simplified way, which further holds back his language development.

The excessively slow 'natural' development of these children and their failure to respond to ordinary educational techniques have led other workers to attempt to develop special acceleration programmes. A research project with young severely retarded children is about to start in Hull under Alan Clarke's direction. This will be an experimental intervention programme, aimed at accelerating development by helping parents to use behaviour modification techniques. The experimental group will be randomly selected from the population of children aged 18 months to $2\frac{1}{2}$ years referred to two local paediatricians because of very slow development. The parents in the experimental group will work for two to three hours per fortnight with the psychologist, and their children's progress will be compared with that of children in two control groups, one of whom will receive advice once a month only, whilst the other will be visited only to assess the children.

Chris Kiernan of the Thomas Coram Research Unit and his associates are also currently working on the application of behaviour modification techniques to the training of pre-school severely retarded children. The special feature of this project is that work will be done with the same child in both home and school, and with both his parents and teachers. This is because experience of parental drop-outs from programmes (if parents are not self-selected volunteers) has led Kiernan to believe that one must work with teachers as well as parents. To assess the effectiveness of this form of intervention the relative rates of development of three groups of children are being examined. Two of these groups currently attend the Hornsey Centre for Handicapped Children. With one group the research team will work with both teachers and parents, with the second group only with teachers, and the third group will receive no special training, although they may be receiving some form of full or part-time pre-school education.

Kiernan argues that the free-flowing structure and content of ordinary nursery school contributes little to the development of young severely handicapped children, who need individualized teaching techniques and initially at least material reinforcements. The content of the syllabus Kiernan offers is dictated by a Gagné type analysis of the step-by-step progression of skills needed. The goals are selected by a functional analysis of the situations the child will be operating in, e.g. the need for communication with the teacher. Children are assessed within the framework of the programme on a teaching orientated assessment battery, covering a range of behaviours from inspection and tracking to communication. The battery was designed and developed for use with profoundly retarded individuals.

A further stage of the work will begin in the autumn. This part of the study will concentrate on an investigation of teaching styles, looking at whether the home or school background of the child can be improved from an operant approach in order to facilitate development. Particular attention will be paid to aggressive and destructive behaviour. It is expected that the research programme will cover home observation of parent–child interaction, investigation into the maintainance and modification of problem behaviour, and ways of teaching and training parents and other adults. On the basis of his study Kiernan hopes to make recommendations for a local community service for young severely sub-normal children.

There are three ongoing research projects at the Hester Adrian Research Centre in Manchester concerned with young severely subnormal children. One, directed by Cliff Cunningham, concerns the development of visually directed reaching in Down's syndrome infants. Videotape recordings of this behaviour are made in the child's home at two-weekly intervals. Reaching was chosen as the first major exploratory skill to develop, after visual searching. Mongols are generally believed to show from an early age a deficit in exploratory behaviour, and Cliff Cunningham would like to find out whether this deficit is related to a general low level of activity, or to the type of parental handling they receive. Later he would like to investigate ways of facilitating this behaviour with the hope of producing long-term effects on the child's acquisition of object permanence and other developmental milestones.

Dorothy Jeffree is currently involved in a more immediately interventionist project—one aimed at assisting parents to facilitate the development of their mentally handicapped child. She plans to work with 25 severely subnormal children, over 18 months of age but under five years, and their parents. On the basis of the assessment which she and the parent will make of the child's development and special needs she plans to design 'teaching games' to facilitate particular intellectual skills in children. Originally each parent and child will be seen for a two-hour session once a week, but she hopes to gradually reduce the number, leaving the parent in charge of teaching his child with the support of occasional home visits. The 'teaching games' when developed should be useful to many other parents and children. Dorothy Jeffree emphasizes that for real progress to be made in helping the child, experts must share their expertise with parents, simply because the parent, in contact with the child all day and everyday, is the only one who can give him sufficient practice in learning skills.

Another 'action research' which is just beginning, under the direction of Cliff Cunningham and James Hogg, involves setting-up and monitoring a pre-school centre which will include both normal and severely subnormal children. Among the questions it is hoped to answer are what is the best ratio of normal to subnormal children, and how can skills best be taught in this group setting?

Both Dorothy Jeffree and Cliff Cunningham have been involved in developing workshop courses of varying length for the parents of mentally handicapped children, which have the aim of helping parents to make a more accurate and objective assessment of their children's development, and giving them some understanding of principles which will help them to alter behaviour and develop skills.

John and Elizabeth Newson with their students at Nottingham are making studies of communication sequences between mongol and deaf babies and their mothers, using videotape recordings. As in their projects with normal children, they see the implications of this work as lying in the relationship between the communication abilities of these children and their cognitive skills. They are also currently running groups for parents of handicapped children in which each parent is helped to work out a remediation programme for their own child in the light of their intimate knowledge of him. Toys are used as the focus for developing skills, and parents are taught behaviour modification principles and encouraged to apply these flexibly in their homes.

II
Important Areas for Future Investigation

INTRODUCTION

All the research workers interviewed were asked not only about their current research, but about their opinions on what are the most important questions in the area of pre-school education in which research should be initiated. In addition, several research and education administrators and trainers of teachers contributed opinions. Naturally, most research workers considered that they were already themselves investigating the key issues. Hence in a sense the first part of this review represents both what is currently being investigated and what investigators working in this field see as the most significant problems.

A number of the suggestions outlined below were not posed as academic research projects, but concerned the introduction of services. It was generally assumed that some form of 'action research' would be incorporated. Some of the problems mentioned are in fact currently being investigated, as reported in the first section of the review.

TOPICS RELATED TO THE EDUCATION OF SOCIALLY DISADVANTAGED CHILDREN

1. Research concerned with assisting young disadvantaged children to acquire skills

A major impetus to the expansion of nursery education has been the belief that school failure can be prevented by early educational intervention. For perhaps the majority of research workers in this field, in Britain as well as in the United States, the problems of early education are mainly conceived in terms of the problems of assisting young disadvantaged children.

At a recent SSRC seminar on Language and Learning it was pointed out that the term 'disadvantaged' is used in at least three ways: (i) to refer to children from certain social groups, e.g. social class IV and V, large families, single parent families, or even residents in certain areas. For the rest of this report these groups will be referred to as 'socially disadvantaged'; (ii) to refer to children who experience learning difficulties at school, leave school as early as possible, and do not enter tertiary education. They cannot, of course, be identified at the pre-school stage. These children will henceforth be referred to as 'educationally disadvantaged'; (iii) to refer to children with certain characteristics, in terms usually of their low scores on language and/or other cognitive tests, which are considered likely to result in school failure. These children will be called 'intellectually disadvantaged'. In fact remediation programmes have usually selected children by demographic variables, mainly social class, and have assumed that such children are likely to have certain language and cognitive deficits and that those are responsible for subsequent school failure. Social, educational and intellectual disadvantage are thus seen as three sides of the same coin.

The extent to which these three kinds of disadvantage are in fact related will be discussed later, under the heading 'characteristics of the socially disadvantaged child' (p. 56). At this stage, however, it is, probably helpful to keep the distinctions in mind; not all investigators appear to have done so, and some of the suggested research topics would have been clearer if the criteria of disadvantage had been specified.

(a) Remediation by nursery school attendance

Many research workers were pessimistic about the likelihood of altering the long-term educational prospects of young socially disadvantaged children, at any rate within the existing education structure. This is because of a widespread disenchantment with the possibility of effecting cognitive changes through nursery schooling, and a general conviction that the family is a much more important influence on early development. Opinions varied as to the possibility of improving the adequacy of parents as educators, but few saw the existing nursery school as likely to play a useful role in parent education. Ann and Alan Clarke regard the nursery school expansion programme as a gigantic social hoax, in so far as it is seen as an important way of combating social deprivation. They argue that there is ample evidence from the USA from 1958 onwards that pre-school education, of the kind we are offering to children, has a negligible effect on their cognitive development and subsequent school achievement. Whilst specially devised nursery curricula may bring temporary cognitive gains, these have invariably been lost once the programme is withdrawn. Long-term reinforcement is difficult to arrange, partly because the type of primary education offered follows the fashion which sanctifies self-generated learning, and avoids the structured approach so essential for the backward and midly retarded. By itself nursery school education can have no direct long-term effects whatever. Moreover, in so far as the expansion programme engenders false hopes of equalizing later opportunity, it may be positively dangerous, since inevitable failure will lead to the same kind of backlash against expenditure on education as has occurred in the USA.

John and Elizabeth Newson are equally sceptical of any cognitive benefit to the child of attendance at nursery schools as they are currently organized. This is not only because of the American work cited by the Clarkes, but because their current experimental work suggests that the communication competence of the child begins to develop in early infancy; for this reason schooling which starts at the age of three may be already too late.

Both the Clarkes and the Newsons suggest that the only type of remediation with any hope of success is intensive daily work on a 1 : 1 basis; the Newsons add that such a programme should begin well before the age of three, and the Clarkes' that it should extend to the age of fifteen. No intensive remedial programmes of this nature are at present under way in this country. In the Newsons' opinion, this work would be more likely to succeed if pre-schools, at least, were based on ordinary houses within the neighbourhood, where parents could 'drop in' informally, and perhaps be influenced by the school activities. This suggestion was made by a number of workers, not only on the grounds that such a centre could more easily be integrated into the local community but also because it was argued that the conventional nursery school or class constitutes too large a unit for the young child to cope with easily, and that it is difficult to develop 1 : 1 relationships between adults and children in large groups and open-plan buildings. Joan Tough suggested that several small pre-school units in ordinary houses could be outposts of the local infant school, to which teaching staff could be attached.

(*b*) *Remediation through work with parents: via parental involvement in school*

A number of research workers believed that socially disadvantaged children could best be helped by influencing their parents. Some saw as the most effective technique for this purpose bringing parents into closer contact with the schools. Parental 'involvement' in schools had however a different meaning and significance for different workers.

Van der Eyken argued that this should be a two-way process. Not only should parents be encouraged to spend time in school, but teachers should be encouraged to spend more time in the children's homes. The traditional nursery school is child-centred; if the parents are involved in discussion with the teachers, the discussion focuses on the child in school. Yet since the mother–child relationship is the key to the whole development of the young child, an important use of the nursery school should be as a base for staff to go out to work with the child in his home.

Others, however, saw the main need as enticing parents into the school, perhaps by the use of videotapes, informal talks, and so on, in order that they can learn from the teachers about child development and the school curriculum (Joan Tough, Peter Wedge). Others argued that parents would only be influenced if they were brought into school in the role of collaborators, at least at the level of discussion (Cashdan, M. Clark). Margaret Clark pointed out that this would involve changing teachers' attitudes to parents as much as parents' to teachers. Too often schools do not know or value what the parents are contributing to the child's education. Cashdan also emphasized that in order to influence parents, the teachers' traditionally hostile and distancing attitude to them must change.

Most of those formerly involved in the EPA pre-school programme (Halsey, Midwinter, Watt) also stressed the importance of drawing parents into the educational process. They now see the educational needs of the disadvantaged child less in terms of the provision of special school experiences or curricula than in terms of re-structuring education so that both the parents and the wider community are drawn into the educational role. This need not necessarily take the form of initiating and organizing the service, as parents have done in the case of play-groups. Other forms of participation could be valuable, including watching and helping in the classroom. Halsey and his colleagues at Oxford would like to see research into a variety of aspects of parental involvement in pre-school education. One approach would be by anthropological case studies of the effect on women's lives of involvement in running a playgroup. How often does it lead to their involvement in other community activities, or to an extension of their activities in other directions? Again, what effects do different kinds of parental involvement in playgroups (e.g. initiating and organizing, or on the other hand spending time watching their children) have on parents' interactions with their children, and of the children's development? Halsey would also like to see a new form of parent involvement—nurseries and creches set up in places of work, in which mothers were allowed time off work to watch and learn about their children. If more women with young children are to be drawn into the labour force it is important to find ways in which they can still be involved in their education.

Marianne Parry and Margaret Roberts would also like to see further study of teacher–parent relationships and of parental involvement in pre-school. How does it work out in practice, and what does it achieve? It would be useful to describe what actually happened in various settings, and which kinds of participation are helpful and which are not. Margaret Roberts would like to see a study mounted to look at the main areas of difficulty between teachers and parents, and the best way of overcoming them in the interests of the child. What is involved in collaboration between parents and teachers? Discussion between teachers and parents who had run their own playgroups would be particularly useful.

Because of their belief in the importance of parental involvement in some form, most of those interviewed were troubled by the tendency of local authorities to increase the number of nursery classes attached to primary schools rather than increase the number of independently-sited nursery schools or playgroups, since they saw little likelihood of real parent involvement in nursery classes as currently organized. However, one administrator at least saw building a relationship between families and schools as an essential part of the nursery expansion programme (Tomlinson).

Bernstein and Bruner are sceptical of the effectiveness of parental involvement in the pre-school which does not include sharing decision-making power with parents. This is because of their belief that parents' interactions with their children are largely influenced by their own role and position in society. Bruner would like to see researchers setting up and running a model pre-school centre with the collaboration of the local community, and describing how it works and the problems it meets.

The kind of parental involvement in schools which different people advocate is closely related to their beliefs about the role boundaries between teachers and the rest of the community. Halsey and others would like to break down these boundaries and to convince both parents and teachers that teachers do not have an exclusive professional expertise. Joan Tough and Margaret Roberts on the other hand insist that the teacher has a professional expertise for which there is no substitute. Joan Tough argues that if what one is trying to do is to improve the thinking skills of young disadvantaged children, it is no use leaving them to develop in a playgroup staffed by disadvantaged mothers, unaware of the cognitive problem and ignorant of how to deal with it. For this reason, to her, parent involvement in the pre-school means primarily parents learning from teachers. The only current study of parent involvement appears to be that of Halsey and Smith (p. 22).

(c) Remediation through work with parents: via home visitors

Opinions also differed sharply about the possible contribution to parent education of home visitors. Bruner and Bernstein are sceptical about such programmes, because of their belief that the curriculum within the family is dependent on very general social attitudes and social realities (c.f. discussion earlier on p. 40). Ann and Alan Clarke argue that those parents most in need of help are least likely to seek it, to accept it if offered, or to alter their behaviour. However, they would support a demonstration experiment of intensive home visiting, where the aim was to work with the mother rather than the child, provided that the experiment was mounted for about fifteen years.

John and Elizabeth Newson have grave misgivings about home visiting schemes. These may in their opinion harm the mother's relationship with the child and hence the child's development, if the mother draws the inference that she had been judged inadequate. Joan Tough is also opposed to home visiting, which she sees as an intrusion on the mother's privacy, and rather similar objections were advanced by Hubbard. Marianne Parry and others pointed out that it would be a very expensive service, and that discussion groups in schools and clinics might be equally effective but much cheaper.

On the other hand, Van der Eyken and Joyce Watt argue that some families are unlikely to take advantage of playgroups and nursery schools or attend clinic meetings and will only be reached by a home visitor. They would like to see experimental programmes set up in this area, using Health Visitors (Joyce Watt) or women with a less official status (Van der Eyken). Tomlinson thought that home visitors might have a useful part to play in building the relationship between home and school, provided they are accepted by mothers as suitable persons to advise them. (Current research in this area was reviewed in the first section, p. 17).

(d) Work with parents: via television

Many people whilst not advocating home visitors felt that most parents of all social classes would welcome more information about child development, and this might well influence their behaviour. Jack Tizard pointed out that at present there is virtually no government sponsored parent education about child development in Britain—Health Visitors and Infant Welfare Clinics largely confine their advice to child health, whilst very little parent education comes from the schools. Bruner, the Newsons and Philip Williams suggested that television could be a very effective educational medium, provided that the programmes were aimed at a really wide audience. Philip Williams was in favour of research funds being allocated for a pilot TV project in parent education, incorporating if possible some attempt to monitor changes in parental attitudes and associated changes in child development. It has been his experience in the Open University in working with TV producers, that it is quite possible to establish a framework of working in which academics collaborate creatively to produce effective and sound programmes. For example, one can agree in advance that 'the experts' should be involved in both the planning and editing stages of the programme.

(e) Work with parents: via classes for adolescents

Educating adolescents for parenthood was mentioned only by Hubbard (who is currently carrying out such a project, see p. 17), Bryan Dockrell and Brian Jackson. Brian Jackson argues that secondary schools too often avoid contact with the world around them and traffic in irrelevant knowledge. Children need to know about motorbikes and hire purchase schemes more than they need to know about medieval history, and they also need to know what is involved in being a parent. Twelve months after leaving school many girls are having babies. These babies are not always unwanted when they are conceived. At this stage girls often believe that motherhood is what they want, but they have no resources to cope with the crying, wetting, demanding real-life child when it arrives. School should confront them with the awkward reality of young children, and also try to teach them something about their needs. He therefore advocates parenthood classes in secondary school, with a mainly practical orientation. Dockrell would like to see a programme developed for ESN children, in which the emphasis was placed not on the physical care of babies but on ways of interacting with babies and young children. Such a programme would need to be developed in conjunction with a nearby nursery. Dockrell points out that the Skodak and Skeels study showed a long time ago that quite retarded girls could in certain circumstances make good foster-mothers; mothercraft training with them might help to prevent retardation in their own children.

(f) Remediation through development of specific educational strategies

Whilst almost no-one interviewed saw nursery school attendance *per se* as likely to result in significant cognitive benefit, a number of people believed that the use of specific educational strategies within the pre-school would help disadvantaged children. The kind of strategy advocated depended on the person's view of the nature of intellectual disadvantage; however, there were no outright advocates of the 'teacher's kit', that is, of ready-prepared scripted material for the teacher to use in the classroom. A pragmatic approach was taken by H. L. Williams, who would like to see a comparison of the effectiveness of several different approaches to the pre-school curriculum, e.g. a Piagetian approach, Joan Tough's dialogue approach, and the Peabody Language Development Kit. He would also like to see a study of whether teacher-directed play could be effective in assisting cognitive development.

Others singled out particular aspects of cognitive behaviour or particular cognitive skills which they thought it important to develop in disadvantaged children. Such an approach is significantly different from that of the earlier remediation programme, which usually involved an all-out drive to improve 'language' or 'thinking' skills. Jack Tizard would like to see a study of strategies for helping children to persist in, and enjoy, difficult activities. Margaret Donaldson would support research specifically directed towards preparation for reading. Too much emphasis has been put, in her opinion, on the perceptual as opposed to conceptual aspects of pre-reading skills. She suspects that being able to think about words and sounds is an important precursor of literacy. Children therefore need to be taught to be reflectively aware of language, not just to use it. They need to understand that the same meaning can be expressed in different words, and they need to be aware of the kind of errors they can make in using language, and how these errors can be corrected. Another important aspect of pre-reading teaching, in her opinion, is helping children to learn what meanings are conveyed by reading in the adult world, e.g. how the postman manages to deliver the letters, what people find out when they look at newspapers, posters, etc. A difficulty which arises at a somewhat later age is that books for beginning readers often confuse and defeat children by the difficult syntax in which they are written, and this too is an area to which psychologists might address themselves.

Wells would like to see a language curriculum in the nursery school based not on language drill but on the organization by the teacher of language-promoting situations. He argues that the child's language is best developed in joint activity between adult and child in which speech plays an essential part. In such activities the child has an opportunity to hear model utterances from the adult in a context in which he is attentive to the child. This educational strategy, whilst very different from a structured 'kit' approach, does demand more systematic work with the child than is usual in the nursery school, in order to ensurethat he takes part in such joint activities.

Bruner points out that before developing educational strategies we need to know much more about what young children use language for, and at a later age what they use reading for. We need to be sure about what language structures they have, and in what situations they can make effective use of them. When this is known, we need to develop strategies to help children use their language skills in a wide variety of situations, including the classroom.

Joan Tough would like to investigate the best ways in which experiences can be fed to children to extend their development. It is not enough for the nursery school to provide children with experiences— the disadvantaged child has not necessarily had fewer or different encounters with the environment than the advantaged child, but meaning has not been put into his experience by adults. The educational task is to give meaning to his experience, and this cannot be done by a structured programme. (There appear to be no current research projects concerned with developing specific educational strategies, although work on curriculum development is reported on pages 5–9).

(g) *Assessment of remediation programmes in the schools*

Two suggestions were made from rather different viewpoints. H. L. Williams pointed out that there is a dearth of standardized tests for very young children and such tests as we do possess were mostly standardized in the USA. Dockrell, on the other hand, argued that we needed to develop other methods of assessing the changes that occur in children subjected to any educational procedures. The apparent failure of some educational programmes or procedures to effect changes may reflect merely the inappropriateness of the measuring instrument. Standardized tests of attainment and intelligence tend to be used because they are at hand, but the changes effected in the child may in fact occur in some other sphere, e.g. the nature of the approaches which the child makes to the teacher, his readiness to turn to books for information, the nature of the questions he asks. Further, he stressed the need to study what actually occurs during an educational programme. If the interest of the teacher or the researcher is confined to the formal aspects of the programme they may fail to observe the learning strategies which the child is developing in the situation. These may in fact be quite inappropriate; since the nature of the dialogue between adult and child is probably of crucial importance in learning there is a need to look more closely at the subtleties of the interaction in the teaching process.

2. Characteristics of the socially disadvantaged child

It was pointed out earlier that the term 'disadvantaged' is often undefined, but that it is usually assumed that social, educational and intellectual disadvantage are closely and indeed causally linked. It is, however, important to give this assumption careful attention. Children of Social Class IV and V, or children from large families or single parent families are clearly disadvantaged with respect to their chances of gaining access to most of the benefits and sources of power in our society, ranging from good health to high income. This social disadvantage undoubtedly tends to be associated with educational failure, but the mechanisms involved are not well understood. There is no direct causal relationship between social class and educational level; nothing in the occupation of a man causes his child to have reading difficulties, and by no means all Social Class IV and V children are school failures. Further, whilst both socially and educationally disadvantaged children tend to score low on psychometric tests, it has by no means been established that their school failure is caused by linguistic or intellectual deficits; this assumption has recently been challenged in many quarters. There is evidence, e.g. that most children who experience reading difficulties have in fact sufficient knowledge of language structure and vocabulary to master reading (of. Hazel Francis, 1974). Hence school failure in the socially disadvantaged may well not be due to their language or cognitive deficits but related to variables which one can broadly characterize as motivational or to do with interests.

Moreover, advocates of the 'cultural difference' theory argue that most socially disadvantaged children do not, in fact, have language or cognitive deficits, and that they come to school equipped with the same ability to reason and the same language structure as middle-class children. Their relatively low scores on standardized tests are in part a reflection of the explicit middle-class bias of the tests—their vocabulary, their stock of knowledge and their understanding of their environment are not less than, but different from, that of middle-class children and middle-class tests constructors. In part also, it is argued that their low scores reflect lack of experience and reinforcement in the role of test respondent. The middle-class child is accustomed from an early age to being asked the kind of questions by his parents to which they already know the answer and receiving praise for participation in the dialogue. This is part of the middle-class home curriculum, but it is also the essence of the test situation.

A variant of this position, argued by Cole and Bruner and I think not incompatible with Bernstein's views, is that although amongst working-class children there is the same range and distribution of linguistic and cognitive ability as amongst middle-class children, working-class children more often than middle-class children fail to use their ability in the classroom. This is not solely because they are inadequately motivated, they also appear to have a real difficulty in transferring the skills they have learnt in other situations to the classroom. This is probably because knowledge has been transmitted to them in a different way, and because they have not been prepared at home for the de-contextualized teaching techniques of school. According to this view, then, socially disadvantaged children are only intellectually disadvantaged in the context of the school's demand for literacy. Lack of motivation also plays a major part in their educational failure.

Since almost all investigators have confined themselves to standardized tests, and have not studied children's cognitive skills in action in either the home or the street or by systematic experimental investigation, we have in fact very little evidence with which to test the cultural deficit—cultural differences controversy. In the area of language, the recent work of Joan Tough and Hazel Francis has indeed shown that Social Class IV and V children have the same language structures available to them as middle-class children, but that the situations in which they put them to use differ. Some investigators see as an important next step further investigation of the skills with which middle-class children and working-class children enter school.

Such an investigation would entail assessing the children in a variety of naturalistic situations in order to see how they function outside the test situation and the classroom. It would also entail the kind of systematic experiments pioneered by Cole with Liberian children, which were directed to finding situations in which the children were able to solve problems which they could not solve within the confines of a standardized test (Cole *et al.*, 1971). From this kind of experiment one might hope to determine the constraints on the children's ability to learn in the classroom. Apart from the recent work of Joan Tough, and Hazel Francis' studies in the infant school, there appear to be no current investigations of these problems. Joan Tough would like to see further study of the advantaged child. She argues that an analysis of the skills which he brings to school, and in particular the way in which these skills are related to school success, would give us a better understanding of the skills we need to teach to the disadvantaged child.

The 'cultural difference' theory outlined above suggests that socially disadvantaged children come to school with different stocks of knowledge, rather than a lack of knowledge, and different cognitive skills rather than cognitive deficits. By implication such a theory gives a much smaller role to experience than the 'cultural deficit' theory, to the extent that it implies that the same cognitive functions will develop in children reared in a great variety of cultures and sub-cultures. However, it seems important to raise the question of the degree to which some social environments may be intellectually handicapping, e.g. there is evidence of definite retardation in young children from very large low-income families, and childminding establishments which rear children in low stimulus conditions. We have very little knowledge of the extent and the way in which these environments effect children's development, since they are not usually available to investigation. Is their development merely temporarily retarded? If so, in what respects? Or is it significantly altered?

3. The transmission of educational and intellectual disadvantage

It was pointed out earlier that we have very little understanding of the mechanisms by which a person's membership of a socially disadvantaged group tends to result in educational and intellectual disadvantage (however defined) for his children. Basil Bernstein sees as the most important current problem that of studying the transmission process within the family in different social classes, that is, the way in which the child acquires and contextualizes basic procedures, and the extent and way in which decontextualizing of them occurs in the family and school. He argues that it is important to study not only language but also non-linguistic aspects of the child's behaviour. Success at school depends amongst other things on a willingness to undertake solitary privatized activity, and to give selective attention to an adult. By what means do middle-class children acquire these characteristics at a very early age? The willingness of a child to work on his own at a jigsaw puzzle may be more significant for later school work than his language habits, and we need to understand how he is socialized very early into different forms of play.

Philip Williams, also, would like to see a study of the way in which learning occurs at home. A detailed study of learning from 12 to 24 months would be particularly interesting in his opinion since this is the period during which social class differences in development emerge. Probably the most productive approach would be to study one or two circumscribed aspects of development in depth over a period of a year or so.

Some people suggested that further understanding of the mechanisms by which social disadvantage is translated into educational and intellectual disadvantage could be obtained by studying those individuals in groups designated as socially disadvantaged (e.g. single-parent families, or the children of unskilled workers) who were in fact happy and successful at school (Ann and Alan Clarke, Margaret Clark, Brian Jackson).

4. Adapting the school to the socially disadvantaged child

The suggestion that school failure in the socially disadvantaged is related not to deficits in the children but to a mismatch between the interests and learning strategies of child and teacher shifts the locus of remediation from the child towards the school. Most remediation programmes for the socially disadvantaged child implicitly support some form of 'deficit' theory, in so far as they set out to lessen the gap between his skills and the requirement of the educational system. However, if the main problem is motivational, that is, if the child fails to learn because school work appears to him irrelevant and without meaning, no account of pre-school language programmes or encouragement to the parent to interact more with the child is likely to prevent reading difficulties. Instead, one might attempt to embed the school skills in the child's interests, or more fundamentally to alter the importance and the meaning of education in the lives of both parents and children. At one level this implies an alteration in much wider aspects of society than are under discussion here. However, even within the framework of the educational system it can be argued that much more could be done to meet the needs of socially disadvantaged children.

The degree to which schools are monocultural has often been pointed out by Brian Jackson. Unless the child comes from a middle-class white family he does not find his own experiences or way of life reflected and recognized at school or indeed in children's books, television, or even advertisements. The surface manifestations of 'monoculturalism' are fairly easy to rectify—reading books like 'Nippers' can be substituted for 'Janet and John', and pictures of children with black as well as white faces can hang in the classroom. The more subtle manifestations of the teacher's hostility to, or ignorance about, the children's out-of-school experiences, in terms of his attitudes to their accent or dialect, and the value the teacher puts on different kinds of experience, art forms, leisure activity, and even food, are much harder to influence.

However, even if the teacher accepts and values the experiences and interests of socially disadvantaged children, there is a further and even more subtle way in which schools may act as disadvantaging agencies. This is in their implicit assumption that all children have acquired the cognitive procedures and learning strategies of middle-class children. Bernstein argues that the current unstructured self-directed learning environment of the nursery and infant school is disadvantageous to working-class children. Although in some ways potentially beneficial to them, e.g. because it enables the culture of the family and community to enter the classroom, in fact it operates to their disadvantage. This is because the 'invisible' pedagogy of the nursery school originated within a section of the middle-class. Its successful operation depends on a variety of back-up procedures which are not in fact present in working-class families, e.g. an elaborated code of communication, a mother who provides access to symbolic form and is acting as a crucial agent of cultural reproduction, and educational support systems which include the mother's own efforts to help her child master the basic skills when necessary. In so far as this pedagogy is unreflectingly institutionalized in school it does not operate to the advantage of the working-class child. There is, then, in Bernstein's opinion, a prime need for pre-school and primary teachers to look at the principles underlying their pedagogy, and to consider its appropriateness for different social groups. Because an apparently class-free environment is provided, it does not follow that there is class-free tuition.

A somewhat similar point was made by a number of other people, but from rather different approaches. Wootton, for example, thinks it important to discover what assumptions teachers make about what children know and how they learn. Working-class children may be less able than middle-class children to take advantage of the learning opportunities offered them in the classroom because they are less experienced in building up meanings from what adults say. Schaffer thinks it would be important to examine in detail maternal teaching strategies and to compare them with teacher strategies. One would take a situation in which both mother and teacher were asked to teach the child a particular task, and try to determine how they structured the teaching situation, and how their methods related to their aims and to their perceptions of the child and the task. If we understood more about the difference between teaching strategies at home and at school we would understand better the extent to which there is a gulf between these two environments for many children. There appears to be no current research in this country in these areas.

TOPICS NOT DIRECTLY RELATED TO THE EDUCATION OF SOCIALLY
DISADVANTAGED CHILDREN

So far the research areas discussed have all been directly related to the problem of educational disadvantage in socially disadvantaged children. The remaining topics to be discussed, whilst they may bear on the problem, were not usually raised in this context. Problems concerning schools will be raised first.

5. Problems of school organization and staff attitudes

Two areas of interest to a number of people were the influence of forms of school organization and of teachers' attitudes on the educational process. Asher Cashdan and Margaret Clark would welcome a study of the difference in teachers' practice in independently sited nursery schools and nursery classes attached to primary schools. Margaret Clark raised the possibility that nursery classes may lay much more stress than nursery schools on preparation for primary school, and that from the age of three children may be expected to arrive at school punctually, attend regularly, etc. Would this in fact meet the needs of the three-year-old, and is it what parents want? Will nursery classes be as wel-coming to parents as some nursery schools are or will the traditional teacher–parent distance be moved back to the pre-school stage?

Cashdan laid stress on differences in teachers' practice that might result from different degrees of autonomy for the teacher in nursery classes and independent nursery schools. Margaret Clark also raised the question of the effect of the size and layout of the unit on teacher practice. However willing a teacher may be to interact with children individually, it may be difficult to achieve in a large group. This is especially true in the new 'open plan' schools where the group effectively consists of 60 children. Often there are physical limitations e.g. no small secluded place for intimate 1 : 1 adult–child or child–child conversations—from this point of view, many children are getting more education at home with their mothers.

Blurton-Jones was concerned about the effect of the size of the unit on the child's behaviour. There is evidence that some children become wild, noisy and aggressive at home after starting nursery school. The size of the unit may well be a relevant factor; no previous society, he points out, has brought up young children in such large single-age peer groups. Jack Tizard would also like to see further study of the effects of different sized groups, and age distribution within the groups. If dialogue with an adult is indeed one of the most powerful educational techniques, then our present school organization may not be the most appropriate for this purpose. He argues that studies to explore the advantages and disadvantages of different ages of transfer to primary school are needed. What happened to the idea of first schools from infancy to the age of eight?

As an administrator, Tomlinson would like to see research into the difference in effectiveness, if any, of full versus half-day schooling, and morning versus afternoon sessions. Does it matter whether children attend nursery school for five half-days or two-and-a-half full-days? A number of people mentioned the importance of investigating the effects of different staff ratios in the pre-school. Margaret Roberts and Maureen Shields would like to compare the effect of improving the staff ratio and providing support for teachers in the form of discussions and joint work with a research team or a College of Education. Most American programmes which have achieved cognitive gains in the pre-school have combined these two features, and it is important to know whether both are equally important.

Joyce Watt and H. L. Williams would like to see further studies of the consequences of different forms and lengths of staff training. Williams points out that assistants may function as educators to a greater extent than is usually recognized. Joyce Watt asks in what way do classes run by nursery assistants differ from those with a trained teacher in charge? What does a teacher do, in fact, that an assistant or playgroup supervisor does not? Another practical point raised was the need to find out whether, and in what way, 'mature' nursery assistants were better than the girls of 18 who are more often employed.

The way in which a teacher's or playgroup leader's beliefs and social attitudes affect her practice was a problem raised by several people (Chazan, Rose, Cashdan and Clark). Cashdan would like to know whether if the teacher's expressed beliefs include an emphasis on developing cognitive skills, this means that her interactions with the children are in fact different from those of teachers' whose priorities lie elsewhere. And is there an interaction between their beliefs and the social class of the children they teach, so that e.g. their aims for middle-class and working-class children are different? Margaret Clark would like to investigate how far the different expressed attitudes to education of teachers or the different training colleges they have attended, affect their practice. This might be done by selecting children in a number of schools according to certain characteristics and seeing how teachers with different expressed beliefs or training background handle these children. Another approach might be to make a study of teacher's practice in different nursery schools with different expressed aims.

Tomlinson pointed out that when considering the effectiveness or otherwise of pre-school education, it may be important to investigate the social values of staff working in this field, and how they regard and are regarded by the children and families with whom they are working. Alan Davies considered that a useful area of study would be that of the attitudes of both staff and children in school to regional accents, syntax and vocabulary. At what stage do children become aware of dialect differences and what attitudes are expressed by staff in terms of overt corrections? Maureen Shields considers that the attitude of the staff to the children and the social relationship set up between them is the key to education at the pre-school stage. This is because the quality of the communication between them depends on the way in which the adult perceives and behaves towards the child, and the way in which the child perceives and behaves towards the adult.

Unless the teacher values the child, conceives of him as a person who is worth listening to, whose thinking and opinions are to be taken seriously, and unless she sees it as important that she make her meanings explicit to him, she is not likely to engage in the kind of dialogue with him from which he will learn an elaborated code.

A number of people mentioned the need to study processes within the nursery school. Carol Lomax, for example, thought that nursery schools may accomplish less than is hoped of them because children most in need of attention from the staff may not receive it, perhaps because they may reject advances. Alan Davies argues that there is a need to know much more about the language of both staff and children in the nursery school. An anthropological approach might be the most useful at this stage, the research worker acting initially at least as a participant observer, or staff assistant, in the school. What is needed is a linguist, whose initial approach would be quite open, but who would hope to be able to make a socio-linguistic analysis. Kevin Connolly would like to tackle the question of what makes a good teacher. What techniques do teachers use? Can one identify styles of teaching and what are their consequences for the child? Current research into the organization of pre-schools and staff behaviour is reviewed on p. 9. Only a very few of the questions raised here are being studied.

6. Transition to primary school

The problems involved in transferring from nursery school to infants school received surprisingly little mention. In the United States a large scale programme 'Project Developmental Continuity' has recently been set-up to tackle this question. In England, whilst the change in teaching methods may be less abrupt, because of our more informal primary schools, the transition is nevertheless difficult and painful for many children. Joyce Watt would like to see a study made of the transition, with the aim of seeing how it could be deliberately structured to help the child, e.g. by more discussion and exchange of information between the schools. Kevin Connolly and Alan Davies would like to see an investigation made of the extent to which the nursery school prepares the child for the demands of the infant school. Davies asks what kinds of language demands are made of children on entering the primary school? What language usages are expected of them? Having focused on the institutional requirements for language in the primary school, it would then be important to see whether the nursery school provides for them, and whether children who have attended nursery school are better or worse equipped to meet these demands than those without pre-school experience.

Tomlinson and Margaret Clark both raised the question of whether infant teachers have different attitudes and expectations to children who have attended nursery schools or classes, and whether children with or without experience of pre-school groups have different needs and expectations which should be catered for. There appears to be no current research in this area.

7. Staff training

Any serious consideration of education must involve a concern with staff training, and although at present there appears to be no research on this topic, a number of people saw it as a key issue. One aspect of the problem, raised by people professionally involved in teacher training (Alan Brimer, Margaret Roberts, Marianne Parry) was the gap between the training of nursery school teachers on the one hand and of nursery nurses and playgroup leaders on the other. Although nursery nurses and playgroup leaders may in fact carry out many of the same functions as teachers, their training is in no sense comparable. Marianne Parry would like to see a new course for nursery nurses with more educational emphasis. It would be intended for women rather older than the usual NNEB recruit and would have a higher status. Another possibility which she suggested would be for nursery nurses, social workers, and teachers to have the first year of their training in common. Joyce Watt would also like to see more joint courses for teachers, social workers, health visitors and nursery nurses. Brimer stressed the inadequacy of the present teacher training, which does not prepare the teacher for the roles of managing and training assistants, or working with parents.

A more fundamental problem raised by Basil Bernstein was that of the content of the courses for nursery school teachers. At present the training they receive gives them no awareness of the way information and skills are being transmitted in the schools or the principles underlying pre-school pedagogy. They are not taught to monitor their own actions or to reflect on which children are gaining what skills from the educational process they offer. Because an apparently class-free environment is provided, it does not follow that there is class-free tuition. Bernstein would put any research funds available in the area of pre-school education into a teacher training project. He would like to see an experimental training course for pre-school teachers set up which would aim to make them aware of their role as agents in the educational process, in the same way that some secondary school teachers are now. The theoretical analysis should be closely linked with practice—perhaps half-a-day should be spent in study, and the other half in the school.

8. Research concerned with the education of severely subnormal children

Chris Kiernan argues that for the mentally handicapped a key area is that of curriculum development. We have very little knowledge of which cognitive steps are critical in development and whether if we teach the young SSN child to acquire them he will in fact be able to generalize his knowledge. Another important theoretical and practical problem is whether we have to programme for training the child in the same skills in two different settings, e.g. home and school, or whether a skill acquired in one setting will generalize to others.

Both Peter Mittler and Joanna Ryan would like to see more study of the language directed to retarded children by teachers and parents. What function does this language serve? How effective is it in shaping verbal and non-verbal aspects of children's behaviour? How effectively does it promote the child's own language? Other neglected research areas mentioned were the study of play, peer interactions, social and emotional development in severely retarded children, and the remediation of behavioural problems.

9. Problems in early school socialization

The great majority of research problems raised in relation to school were concerned with the development of linguistic and pre-literate skills. However, several people pointed out that other aspects of school life have been neglected for a long time. Connolly would like to see more attention given to the development of motivation. Bruner raised several specific questions related to socialization. Who does the child see as supporting him, and what are the effects of this concept on his learning? How does he see school, and in what way, if any, does he see it connecting with his out-of-school life? How are values passed on to children, and by whom, in present day society? It is clear that much of a child's socialization does not occur within the nuclear family—how does he learn, for example, to handle his own or other's aggression, and how does he develop his characteristic network and mode of expression of sympathy and concern? In both these respects children often differ so widely from their parents that socialization processes outside the family must be operating.

Margaret Manning and Jack Tizard would like to see work done on behaviour problems of children in the nursery school. Some schools, because of the families they serve, have to care for a number of very difficult, usually aggressive, children. Margaret Manning would like to investigate methods and techniques of dealing with aggressive children of different types. For example, 'teasing' children sometimes seem unable to approach other children in a friendly way, even though they would like to be in the 'in group', and it may be possible to help them to improve their social relationships. Jack Tizard suggests that appropriate behaviour modification techniques might well be useful with these children—the large amount of attention which they usually get from the teachers may have a reinforcing effect on their behaviour. The only current work in this area appears to be that of Margaret Manning (p. 16).

10. Problems in early cognitive development which relate to education

Almost all the research topics suggested concerned with cognitive development were raised in the context of assisting the disadvantaged child or of comparing the development of children in different social classes. However, some people raised in a more general way the need to understand the processes by which learning occurs in the early years, or the ways in which cognitive skills can be developed. Several people mentioned the importance of studying the role of play in early learning, and the functions of different kinds of play (Bruner, Parry, Watt).

Marianne Parry would like to see studies of how the child's experiences and activities in the first two years of life lay the foundations of later skills. What happens to children who lack these experiences, e.g. children who are not given toys or children with various kinds of handicap? Chris Kiernan raised a similar question from a sceptical standpoint—how much significance does early behaviour have for later development? There is considerable current stress on the importance of mother–infant interaction, but do we know how much variance it accounts for in later development?

Joan Tough and Maureen Shields would like to know more about the way in which adults structure children's thinking, and how the fundamental cognitive advances are made by the child. We as yet know very little of what young children are capable of—what can we teach a child of three or four? Both Peter Bryant and Margaret Donaldson would like to see educational strategies developed which would use and extend the reasoning abilities of young children. Maureen Shields sees as the most important gap in our knowledge an understanding of how communication systems are set-up between adult and child, and child and child, from a very early age.

11. The general provision of services for the under-fives

A number of people pointed out that the educational needs of under-fives must be seen in a much broader context than that of the formal educational system. Poverty, poor housing, over-crowding, poor maternal health and maternal depression all threaten children's health, development, and family relationships in rather obvious ways. The question of how these ills should be prevented is outside the scope of this review, but a number of those interviewed stressed that any sane society would give priority to these measures.

(a) The contribution of health services

Several people stressed the particular contribution which improved health services could make in the prevention of retardation. Ann and Alan Clarke argue that there is a strong probability that a majority of grossly deprived children are unplanned and unwanted. The first priority should be to attempt to ensure that contraceptive procedures are used and that no child is born unwanted. This should be of top priority for social workers in deprived areas, and would involve not just drawing attention to the existence of Family Planning Clinics but taking advice directly into the home. Research should identify the problems and something like this has been going on in Aberdeen. Where mishaps occur, the first line of defence should be voluntary abortion on social grounds. Failing this, the voluntary offer of the child for adoption should be discussed with the mother.

Martin Richards argues from his research on mother–infant interactions that a wide range of pre- and post-natal medical factors influence child behaviour, e.g. prematurity, obstetric complications and malnutrition, and that improved obstetrical services might do as much for the disadvantaged child as any psychological measure. He believes that useful research could be done in this area.

(b) The safety of children

Brian Jackson argues that considerations of children's safety comes before consideration of their education. One aspect of their safety is the need to protect them against neglectful or cruel parents. We need to make a study of the legal position of children and establish what their rights are, and what people consider they should be. This problem has recently come to public notice because of the lawsuits over compensation for thalidomide children and the tug-of-war cases between foster mothers and natural mothers. How far does biological parenthood give you ownership of a child? One suggestion which should be examined is that in cases of this kind children should have their own advocates to represent their interests in court.

The issues are, however, much wider than legal ones. Children have rights against their parents, against institutions and against society, which often ignores them as persons. Should mothers have the right to work twelve hours a day and leave their children in totally inadequate circumstances? How can we make society aware of the needs of young children when services for adults are developed? The roads have become safer in recent years for adults, but the number of road deaths and accidents involving young children has increased. This means that we are creating a traffic environment which is more dangerous than before for children, and such attempts to modify this trend as the Green Cross Code (Splink) are almost comically ill-informed about what children understand and how they behave. Deaths and accidents of children under five by poisoning are increasing. Again, this is because we put the profits of industry and the comforts of adults before the safety of children. It would be relatively easy and inexpensive to dispense medicine in child-resistant packages, and to make it a statutory requirement for houses to be fitted with lockable medicine cupboards with sloping tops. Before offering the young child schools, we have to investigate ways of offering him health and life.

(c) Group care of under-fives outside their home

A large number of people interviewed expressed anxiety about the apparently inflexible form which the nursery education expansion programme was assuming. It looked as though a service was being set up, and often being given permanent form in the shape of new buildings, almost without reference to the real needs of children and their parents. For a mother who is not working, the prime need may be to free her long before the child reaches the age of three from the 24-hour care of her child, and to involve her in some activity outside her home. Neither of these needs is usually met by nursery school. Blurton-Jones argued that playgroups run by mothers may be much more beneficial than schools. The prime aim of pre-school education should be to improve the quality of the mother–child relationship, and playgroups are likely to be more effective here than schools. At the least, services should be set up with some regard to the preference of mothers, e.g. with respect to hours, flexibility of attendance, and size of the group. Martin Richards also argues that the provision of pre-school services should have as its aim an improvement in the quality of the relationship between young children and their mothers, and that there are more effective ways to do this than by setting up nursery classes. Mothers with young children are under considerable stress in our society; baby-battering is the tip of the iceberg of unhappiness and friction. He would like to see large numbers of small centres set up, where babies as well as small children could be left for a few hours a day in order to give mothers some relief. Joanna Ryan felt that the provision of nursery classes does little to integrate the child and his mother into the community. Yet often both are unhappy because of their isolation. She suggested that ordinary houses should be taken over and used as Young Children's Centres, where parents could leave children for varying periods of time, and also stay with them if they wished. If the centres were also in part community centres for the locality, parents would be more readily attracted to them.

Not only are nursery schools an inadequate solution to the problem of mothers at home, they also do not solve the problem of the care of children of working mothers. Brian Jackson wants more research into childminders: he estimates that about 300,000 young children are being cared for by illegal childminders. This is by no means a problem peculiar to the immigrant groups, since large numbers of both the children and minders are white. Rather, it is an aspect of a society where women with young children go out to work, but no adequate provision is made for the care of their children. Marianne Parry argued that it was particularly important to ensure that children who are away from their mothers for most of their working hours are reached by educationalists. She would like to see research into the best strategies for combining day-care and school facilities for the under-fives.

Eric Midwinter urged that provision for the under-fives should combine flexibility with coherence. Services should be planned in concert with health and welfare services. Because of the tiny catchment area for pre-school provision, 'local diagnosis' of needs is required. It is essential to find some quick, preferably simple, measuring rod for assessing needs and finding solutions. In order to plan services, we need to discover numbers, type of demand, shopping and leisure patterns (the supermarket nursery may be called for), working patterns with reference to shift times (perhaps a factory nursery is needed most), short-run journey networks, and whatever else might be needed for an 'under-five' social profile of that district. Only when armed with this information would it be possible for a pre-school organizer to plan the under-five operation appropriate to that situation. Obviously, for a number of reasons, a liaison with neighbouring places with a similar diagnosis would make for an effective impact. What is almost certainly needed is a very flexible plan not tied to elaborate building programmes, which can be adapted to the changing needs of a community, and ways of evolving such a programme need to be investigated.

A valuable programme of action-research, therefore, might be:

(i) To select a 'honeycomb' of such districts (for instance 10 districts by 5,000 = 50,000) or a large new housing estate;

(ii) To conduct an intensive survey and analysis;

(iii) To map and pilot a solution.

Hopefully, the survey and analysis would provide a formula for general use, whilst the pilot solution would demonstrate the merit of the concept. (Jack Tizard is currently directing a project which fulfils most of these requirements, as described on page 41). Such a project calls for the coordination of a variety of services. Jack Tizard pointed out that the effect of having a number of separate government departments concerned with services for the under-five is dysfunctional and the development of separate programmes by these departments is bizarre. Different problems even arise at the working level, due to the superior salary, conditions and prestige of teachers. A unified service which will consider all the needs, including health needs, of under-fives is required. He thinks we need as many pre-school centres as there are infant schools. A number of people asked for further information on services, which in some districts at least is currently being collated (cf. Joyce Watt's project, p. 37).

Halsey would like to know more about ordinary pre-school play-groups. What kind of children attend them, and to what extent and in what way are parents in fact involved in running them? How many function in working-class districts, and how successfully do they draw in working-class mothers? Others have asked for information about the characteristics of the children who are filling the places in the new nursery classes—do the children in most need of education receive it?

Peter Wedge sees as an important area for research the evaluation of new services, and the description of the organizational problems they bring. What are the effects of providing a service for young children on the child's development, and what impact does it have on the families it serves and on the local community? Clearly, the findings are not necessarily generalizable from one area to another, since the effects may vary according to the characteristics of the area, and also according to the way in which the service is set up and run, e.g. the part the parents play in running it. The long-term evaluation of the effect of different types of pre-school provision on children's development was mentioned only by Cashdan.

(d) The need for services for young handicapped children

Maurice Chazan, Margaret Clark and Jack Tizard drew attention to the pre-school needs of handicapped children, including deaf and physically handicapped children. Jack Tizard argued that serious attempts should be made to integrate these children into ordinary schools and provide the extra staff and facilities needed to make this feasible. Such integration is especially important for young children who would otherwise have to make long journeys to a specialized unit, or even attend boarding school. Joanna Ryan argued that the provision of services for families with young severely retarded children was a much more pressing need than psychological research about them. Their mothers need a great deal of support of all kinds, including playgroups or other forms of day care.

(e) Pre-school services for the children of immigrants

Other groups in need of special attention are the children of West Indian and Asian immigrants. Halsey points out that West Indian children appear to enter school at a particular disadvantage and it is important to try to find the kind of pre-school service which helps the children best and is most acceptable to their mothers. Children of Asian parents have different needs again; they need help in learning the English language and customs, and particular skills and knowledge are needed on the part of staff to help their mothers venture outside their family environment.

III
General Issues Raised in Discussion

As well as asking for opinions on the important areas in which research should be initiated, I raised in discussion two general questions. One of these, the manner of allocating research funds, is of particular interest to research workers, but the second, the manner of communicating and implementing research findings, is of concern to both research workers and consumers of research.

THE COMMUNICATION AND IMPLEMENTATION OF RESEARCH FINDINGS

This is a topic which aroused strong feelings; fundamentally it raises the problem of the separation between theory and practice in the allocation of roles in our society—those who study education are separate from those who carry out education—indeed, the latter are often the object of study of the former. The consequences of this division were put most savagely by Brian Jackson, who argued that research tends to be an almost entirely internal process. On the one hand it is a device for keeping research workers in a job and increasing their status and income. At the same time it provides raw material for students to write essays and theses about. But often nothing in the real world changes as a result of the research. This is because since research workers are not involved in the educational process they tend to tackle out-of-date, irrelevant or trivial questions. To the extent that they are aware of their alienation from practice they often feel parasitic or voyeuristic.

Marianne Parry described research from the teacher's point of view. Often research problems appeared remote from the teacher's job, or else irrelevant to her problems. Usually the teacher's only contact with research is someone arriving at school, distributing questionnaires, perhaps observing or testing her children, and then disappearing for good. Marianne Parry considered that the only way in which research workers could influence teachers was by the investigation of problems which they could show to be relevant to the teacher and by bringing teachers into the research team from the beginning. The same point was made by J. Tomlinson, H. L. Williams,

Joyce Watt and Joan Tough. Geoffrey Matthews would go further. Any educational research unit needs, in his opinion, a large corpus of interested teachers who will try out ideas as they are formulated and help to shape them. He would also argue for the importance of a new profession of 'research teacher', drawn either from the ranks of research workers or teachers, who would regularly spend part of the week in classroom teaching, trying out the application of their ideas themselves. Joan Tough is in favour of induction courses for any research worker intending to do research into pre-school education; six months should be spent observing and if possible working in the schools before formulating research projects about them.

Bryan Dockrell and Chris Kiernan, like Matthews, felt that the researcher must himself be at times a practitioner. Dockrell argues that for anyone who wants to influence teachers' practice, being able to carry out the practices you recommend is important. Kiernan made the further point that not only does the research worker gain credibility by this rolling up of sleeves, but also a better understanding of the major variables that influence the situation he is studying. A number of people argued that the participation of teachers in research was not only an essential part of communicating with them, but the most effective way of changing them. Margaret Clark and Asher Cashdan were sceptical about the effectiveness of refresher courses in altering teachers' attitudes and practices. Asher Cashdan thinks there is evidence that teachers gradually revert to their former practice after the course ends, and Margaret Clark suspects that those teachers who appear to be influenced by special courses are those whose attitudes and practices were similar in the first place to those in charge of the course. In her opinion, the most effective way of influencing teachers is by getting them involved in working out a programme of educational change. Margaret Roberts points out that professional research workers, who in any event are in very short supply, are not necessary for this purpose; Colleges and Institutes of Education can stimulate teachers and improve their understanding by working with them in the schools on research projects. Time and resources, however, need to be allocated by the authorities to make this possible.

Not all research workers were prepared to bridge the gap between research and teaching by altering their roles, but almost everyone recognized the need for more effective written communication of research findings. Marianne Parry pointed out that even when research is relevant to teachers' needs, researchers are often unsuccessful in explaining their findings. Not only do their concepts need more explanation, but they tend not to put their research into a context which makes it relevant or meaningful to the teacher. In addition, their writing tends to be replete with unattractive statistics and graphs. Marianne Parry suggested that a 'research interpreter' might be appointed, who would translate research ideas and findings in an intelligible form. Bruner suggested setting up a centre, or 'think-tank', with the specific aim of helping researchers communicate their findings effectively.

Philip Williams suggested that the University might provide brief courses to help research workers improve their communication style. Tomlinson, the Clarkes and Gordon Wells all suggested that bodies which commission research, such as the SSRC, should accept responsibility for interpreting and disseminating research findings. Part of the research grant might be set aside for this purpose, and perhaps used to pay a scientific journalist. Jack Tizard, whilst recognizing the problem, wondered how much responsibility the research worker should himself take for this task, which would seriously impinge on his research time. Brian Jackson advocates 'open research', that is, communicating your research ideas and findings as you go along. This has the effect that your research is not private: a lot of other people will move into your area of interest and 'steal' your ideas. Moreover, you make your mistakes in public. On the other hand, it is a very effective way of communicating with and influencing the public.

Both Jack Tizard and Halsey raised the question of the need for better communication between research workers, and between research workers and academic staff. Jack Tizard argued that there is a serious need for a social sciences equivalent of the *British Medical Journal*, i.e. a weekly paper in which findings can be briefly reported. Halsey would like to see a Dissemination Centre in the DES which would collate and disseminate the results of educational research. A great deal of research work is wasted if the dissemination of findings is left to chance. It would also be very useful if there was some organization which mapped and monitored research and service development, so that one could find out, for example, where home visiting programmes were going on or what new developments there were in community education. Bruner suggested that funding bodies could spend quite small amounts of money in a useful way by organizing meetings and workshops for people working on similar problems.

Most people saw communicating with administrators as a rather different problem. Jack Tizard pointed out that at the present time many administrators are interested in and receptive to research findings. There is, however, a grave danger of 'over-sell', of promising more than one can fulfil. Bryan Dockrell thought that it was often desirable to urge caution, and to suggest that a new policy inspired by research findings should be tried out in a limited way, or using a model. In Dockrell's opinion, communication with administrators is not the responsibility of the research worker: someone needs to stand between the research worker and the administrator to interpret the administrative implications of research findings and discuss policy with administrators in the light of research findings. A very different point of view came from Chris Kiernan who raised the problem of how to influence administrators who were unwilling to accept ideas. One solution that might more often be attempted in his opinion is for researchers to move into executive positions in order to implement their ideas, that is, actually to take responsibility for their recommendations, and not just give advice to others. This would also give the further advantage that the researcher is in a better position to experiment and try out his ideas in practice. Tomlinson suggested that administrators, like teachers, would be easier to influence if involved in discussion about research from the planning stage onwards. Study groups to discuss research findings, which should include local educational authority advisers, administrators, teachers, and members of the staffs of Colleges and Institutes of Education would be a useful innovation.

HOW SHOULD RESEARCH FUNDS BE ALLOCATED?

There was no general agreement on this issue. Joan Tough argues that the important research problems needing investigation are best tackled by carefully investigating small numbers of children. An ideal research centre concerned with innovation in the pre-school might be one where a number of small projects were being carried out by different investigators, and evaluated by an independent psychologist. Large-scale programmes involving large numbers of children are unlikely to advance knowledge in the important areas. Bruner and Margaret Donaldson also would prefer to see research money put into small-scale projects. Margaret Donaldson recognizes that for some purposes large programmes are necessary, but she thinks there is an unfortunate tendency in the academic world for a person's prestige to be related to the size of the research grants which he holds. This is apt to cause people to spend so much time negotiating grants, writing reports and supervising assistants that they have relatively little time left for thinking about the research problem or working on it themselves. There are cases where it would be better to do without a grant—or to have a much smaller one—and to work with research students. In this way the research worker gains by maintaining more direct involvement, and the students may benefit from the working partnership. It should be stressed, though, that there are dangers in this for the students unless the research worker is scrupulous about not taking advantage of them.

Margaret Donaldson wonders whether we might not do more about giving research money on a fairly loose rein to people who can be identified as creative and productive, thus leaving them free to go where the problems lead them, instead of having to set up vast 'programmatic' structures in advance. She does not mean to suggest that these should replace other methods of funding research, only that it merits consideration as an additional way of encouraging interesting work. Brian Jackson also would like to see funding bodies prepared to give funds on a much looser rein. The research worker is expected at an early stage to define specific questions, define samples, and name locations. This does not allow him time to spend finding out about the problems he is investigating, perhaps working in the field in which he is interested in some humble role. But this time is the 'thinking space' of his project, and if it is not allowed for adequately the research may be an expensive waste of time.

Ann and Alan Clarke on the other hand argue that rather than squandering public money on a lot of little projects, often conducted by mediocre research workers, it would be better to select teams of first-class experimental scientists and invite them to pursue a thorough programme of long-term research. The apparent divergence of these views may be reconciled by Jack Tizard's opinions on research funding. His experience with the SSRC and MRC has led him to the conclusion that the most effective research comes from two types of funding—centres, or units, which are guaranteed at least a six-year life, and which bring together a number of scientists working, perhaps independently, in the same area, and small grants to individuals of up to four or five thousand pounds. The medium size grant running for three years tends to be unsatisfactory—the work is not followed up, and it is difficult to attract any except junior staff because of the brief tenure. Hence there is a considerable shortage in Britain of research staff who have had five years or so of research experience.

However, research units are inevitably costly to set up and run. One with a scientific staff of seven will cost in the region of £50,000 a year and the social services so far appear unwilling to face up to the financial implications of organizing serious research. Such units would need to develop a working relationship with a universtiy; staff should have the option of being absorbed into the university when the unit disbands, and in return the unit should give lectures and supervise students.

IV
Concluding Remarks

The reader who has reached this point is likely to feel overwhelmed by the number and variety of research projects under way or suggested, all of which appear to have some degree of interest or merit. With respect to a decision about research priorities, the reader is on his own. There was no single issue which was generally agreed by those working in the area to be the most significant; the only common ground amongst all those interviewed was a degree of dissatisfaction with the nursery education expansion programme in its present form.

The wide range of problems which were suggested is due in part to the fact that any research worker worth his salt can (and did) suggest half a dozen 'interesting' projects when asked to do so. In part, also, it stems from the different working roles of the people interviewed, e.g. administrators are more likely to be concerned with the organizational aspects of education than its content, trainers of teachers tend to give more weight to problems of schools and teachers than do people working with parents, whilst research workers studying cognition are more likely to be concerned with the learning process. More fundamentally, though, the lack of consensus is related to certain basic differences in attitude.

The first of these concerns the extent to which people's interest extends beyond the formal educational system. For some, the issue of over-riding importance is the need to develop adequate services to improve the quality of life for young children and their parents. There is an increasing amount of documentation that the years when their children are under the age of five impose most strain on the mental health of women, and their marriages. At this time family income is at its lowest (except for the period of retirement), housing is at its least adequate, and women are expected to undertake the 24-hour care of their children at the most demanding stage of their development. In present-day urban society women usually receive very little support in this role from the community, or in many cases from their own families and husbands. The resulting high rate of mild depression and marital strain, particularly in working-class women, impairs family relationships and communication and thus provides a poor educational environment for young children. The first need, in the opinion of many people, is to provide services which will reduce the isolation of mothers and their children from the period of infancy onwards, by drawing them into community life, and which will also give mothers some relief from their 24-hour responsibility.

A rather different priority which is also educational in the broader sense is to provide adequate care for the children of working mothers. There is an increasing tendency for women with young children to go to work: the fact that this tendency is apparent in all social classes and in most countries, and that it is steadily increasing, suggests that the motivation is not solely financial.[4] Indeed, those Eastern European countries which offered a 'mother's wage' to mothers of young children who would stay at home found few women willing to accept the offer. For a variety of reasons, the children of working mothers are often reared in a environment which should be considered totally unacceptable in contemporary Britain—with frequent changes of childminders, a very inadequate amount of adult attention, a dearth of toys or other objects to play with, no opportunity for running about, no stories or picture books. The provision of a lavishly equipped half-day nursery school even in the same road may not begin to meet these children's needs, since the childminder may well not make the effort to get the children clean and dressed at the right time to take them to and from school.

Many people thus see the nursery school in its present form as a hopelessly inadequate solution to the educational needs of those families who most need help. It neither meets the needs of the mother to be integrated into the local community and to have the possibility of an hour or two of relief from her baby or toddler, nor does it meet the needs of the working mother.

As an alternative to increasing the numbers of nursery schools and classes, some of those interviewed urged that we should develop Children's Centres, to serve a small community, organized perhaps with the assistance of local community groups, where mothers and young children could meet, and children could be cared for without their

[4] A survey in 1973 of 978 children aged $3\frac{1}{2}$ in S.W. England and S. Wales showed that the mothers of three out of ten of the children were working, and that there were no social class differences in the proportion of working mothers (unpublished findings from A. Osborne, 'Child Health and Education in the Seventies').

mothers, either all day or for short or occasional periods of time. Because the needs of localities change over time, e.g. the children on a new estate grow up, and there are fewer new babies, the services should be planned flexibly and not tied to expensive one-purpose buildings. Indeed, there are many reasons for arguing that one or two local houses, or flats in a block of flats, have distinct advantages over larger purpose-built centres. Both mothers and young children may feel more at home in them, and the small size of the rooms may tend to encourage smaller groups and more 1 : 1 adult–child interactions. But any development of this kind is difficult or impossible as long as the responsibility for services for under-fives is divided amongst different government departments.

A second and related basic issue on which those interviewed were divided was the extent to which they saw pre-school education as dependent on the expertise of the professional teacher. Because the main and continuing educational influence on the child is his family, many people see as the most significant educational need for the under-fives not bringing them in to the formal educational system, but developing methods by which parents can become more efficient educators. There is considerable disagreement over the methods. Some people advocate direct parent teaching by one of a variety of techniques, e.g. home-visitors, watching and helping teachers, classes in clinics or schools, TV programmes. Others argue that the way in which parents interact with their children depends on very general aspects of their life and their position within society, e.g. the pressures of poverty and overcrowding, ill-health and fatigue, feelings of power-lessness and of alienation. From this point of view, changes in the family's material conditions and changes in the class structure of society are seen as the basis for changing communication and education within the family.

For a variety of reasons, therefore, many of those interviewed saw the problems of what kind of schooling to provide for the under-fives as relatively trivial compared with the need to improve the educational influences on the child outside the school system. However, to the extent that the tendency for children to spend more time from a younger age in group care appears to be increasing, the problems of curriculum development cannot be avoided. Within the family, pre-school education occurs incidentally, mainly as a consequence of the child sharing the activities and interests of the rest of the family. This is not to say that there is not an implicit pedagogy and an invisible curriculum in the home; indeed, middle-class mothers may organize the child's environment with a deliberate educational aim.

Mainly because of work stemming from Bernstein's formulations, we have developed in the last fifteen years a much clearer notion of the way in which as a result of different learning experiences at home children from different social classes arrive at school more or less adequately equipped to learn from the schooling provided. If we are going to look after children outside their homes, we have to make deliberate decisions about the learning experiences we provide, or at the least we must examine the implicit curriculum which underlies the organization of the nursery day. A widespread desire to improve the school attainments of working-class children has led to considerable dissatisfaction with the 'traditional' nursery school regimen. In so far as this regimen was ever considered to be 'compensatory', the rationale was that children needed experience with the rich and varied environment provided as a foundation for symbolic knowledge and skills. The extent to which adults are needed to give meaning to the child's experience was not sufficiently recognized.

Bernstein (1974) has pointed out that the 'invisible' pedagogy of the nursery school is tailored to meet the needs of certain sectors of the middle-class. It provides the middle-class child with experiences he may lack at home (notably, the experience of mixing with a peer group and of enjoying a wide range of athletic and 'messy' activities) whilst freeing him from the continuous supervision of his mother and from over-close dependence on her. At the same time the massive back-up from home provides the child with the opportunity to develop the vocabulary, the functions of language, the meanings, and the attitude of selective attention to an adult which he will need in primary school. On the other hand, because most working-class children (although not all) escape at a very early age into the peer group of the street, or courtyard, they are in less need of the socializing opportunities and freedom to explore offered by the nursery school. For them, however, there are no tutorials at home to supplement the nursery school curriculum. Moreover, whilst at school they are less likely than middle-class children to avail themselves of the opportunities which exist for dialogue with adults, storytelling, and so on, because of their preference for outdoor play with their peers.

For these kinds of reasons, then, even those people interviewed who saw as a priority the extension of the nursery school system considered that some modification of the regimen was needed. Some people would like to develop compensatory language programmes as an adjunct to the play methods of school, in order to develop in the child the skills and concepts which it is believed he needs to succeed in primary school. Others, whilst reluctant to return to formal teaching in the pre-school, believe that the same end could be obtained if the teacher interacted more systematically with those children most in need of dialogue with her. So far this apparently reasonable course has met with some success in terms of temporary increased scores on standardized psychological tests, but has rarely resulted in improved competency at primary school. There are too many unknowns in the process to permit a definite explanation of this failure at the present time. Because the only measures of change available in most compensatory projects are test scores, we do not know what in fact the child learned. It may be that what the child was learning was not the general cognitive and language skills which the programme was seeking to impart, but a skill of relatively trivial importance, that of greater ease in the role of test respondent. Alternatively, he may have learned a more specific skill than was intended, and failed to transfer it to other situations.

Another possibility, however, is that success or failure at school is related to quite other aspects of the child, e.g. his interests and motives. Thus although there was rather general dissatisfaction with the traditional nursery school regimen, there was no general agreement about whether a 'compensatory' element should be built in to it for socially disadvantaged children. Some people are reluctant to accept the widely held view of socially disadvantaged children as psychological deficit systems. They urge that a certain caution must be used in drawing conclusions from the child's poor performance at school and on standardized tests. It does not follow that failure in a specific kind of situation implies lack of ability: it may be that the child does not choose to use, or for reasons which need to be investigated finds it difficult to use, his ability in the school situation. However, there are more theories than investigations in this area. We are still without an adequate picture of the knowledge, capacities and modes of intellectual functioning of children from different social groups, and of how they match or fail to match the intellectual and motivational demands of primary school. In brief, we do not know why working-class children are less successful at school than middle-class children.

From this point of view many see as the most important area to be investigated the transmission process at school as well as at home, and the way in which the interests, and styles of thought and learning of the child may match, or fail to match, those of the school. There is the possibility that the antecedents of school failure lie in the school, rather than the child, and that it is the teacher rather than the child who needs to develop new skills. The pedagogy of the school has so far received almost no study, yet we have good reason to believe that what children learn is only loosely related to what the teacher believes is being taught. Henry Nathan (1973) has emphasized that in learning there is no equivalence of input and output—'most effects are unintended, most understanding is tacit, most communication is subliminal, most knowledge is skill'. Much of the basic socialization of the child is learnt very early without explicit teaching, e.g. sex and social class roles. At school, whilst the teacher is apparently teaching one thing, the child may learn another. What a child learns from an arithmetic lesson, e.g. may be more a sense of inadequacy than an understanding of mathematical concepts.

A further issue on which people are divided is whether in fact we understand enough about cognitive development to devise compensatory programmes. Some people argue that until we know more about the way in which experiences result in learning we cannot devise effective educational techniques. They therefore see as the main research priority the need to understand how the fundamental cognitive advances are made by the child, and the manner and the extent to which experience unlocks the developing capacities of the child. The current interest in infant development reflects this approach; the findings have as yet hardly been assimilated by pre-school educationalists, but the emphasis on the extent to which the child initiates learning and on the degree to which early learning is embedded in significant meaning have implications for later education. So too has the analysis of the considerable intellectual powers of young children, which are hardly matched by such educational aims as the teaching of colour names.

One topic which was raised by very few was a discussion of curriculum development in relation to the goals of pre-school education. For many there was an implicit assumption that the main goal should be the prevention of educational failure. As this report records, the great bulk of current research is concerned with developing language skills in the under-fives; there is virtually no current research concerned with the development of social, artistic or physical skills. The first concern of most psychologists at present is to attempt to equip children with the skills they will need to become literate and numerate, and nursery school is thus widely seen as a 'head-start' for primary school.

In so far as the rest of the educational system, supported by society at large, is primarily concerned with developing literacy and numeracy, there is a widespread feeling that for maximal efficiency and to ensure justice the process cannot be started too early.

However, some psychologists see as one of the great strengths of the traditional nursery school movement the fact that it has never subscribed to such narrow aims. Whilst acknowledging the need of some children for assistance in developing language skills, they express a certain anxiety lest the broader goals of pre-school education should be forgotten. In this they have the support of many parents, whose first concern, at any rate in the early years, is that their children should be happy; they have an uneasy suspicion that too much stress on preparation for primary school will deprive children of their 'playing years'. The broader goals of pre-school education are defined in a variety of ways—thus Chris Kiernan suggested that all education, including pre-school education, should aim at producing autonomous persons, who were sufficiently informed, self-reliant and competent to make decisions. Others would stress the need to develop such qualities as self-confidence, sympathy, respect for others, co-operativeness, imagination, or artistic creativity.

In marked contrast to the work which has been put into language education, these broader goals have not been the subject of curriculum development or research. The traditional nursery school movement has assumed that they are best achieved by a curriculum of self-directed play. The validity of this claim has never been tested. How much knowledge do we have of the steps to take to increase co-operativeness amongst children? We want our children to be happy, but do we really know which kinds of educational environment promote happiness in different children? How do we set about promoting self-confidence in a three-year-old? How do we discourage aggressive behaviour, whilst enabling the child to cope in the unprotected environment of the street or playground? How can we encourage persistence in the face of difficulty? Psychologists have tended to ignore such questions, but they would seem to have at least as much educational importance as, e.g. the development of pre-reading skills.

Because of the assumption that learning in the first five years should be self-directed, apart, perhaps from compensatory programmes for some children the cognitive content of the pre-school curriculum has also received little discussion. The challenge which was laid down by Bruner in relation to education generally has not been taken up in the pre-school; that is, how can we increase the child's power of thought by inventing for him modes of access to the empowering techniques of the culture? How can we convert bodies of knowledge and skill into a form capable of being learned by a young child? Children's intellectual capacities are considerable, and if the objectives to be taught are clearly stated and the skills needed to obtain them clearly specified, we know that surprising competence in a variety of fields can be attained very early. The violin-teaching technique of Suzuki is a case in point. As Susan Isaacs pointed out forty years ago, children are powerfully motivated not only to play but to find out about the world and to develop skills. The strong interest which most children have in, for example, animals, food, motor cars and stories could serve as a powerful lever to bring aspects of biology, physics, mathematics and history within their grasp. The acquisition of physical skills, for example, swimming and gymnastics, can give them more, not less, satisfaction in their play.

The traditional nursery school movement has always stressed that cognitive goals cannot be clearly separated from non-cognitive ones, and in this they are surely right. Such qualities as happiness, self-confidence, and friendliness, as well as their obverse, usually develop as unintended effects of other situations. In the present day nursery school most children appear happy and are absorbed for much of the time in activity which is meaningful to them. There are no failures, and children do not learn that they are inadequate. One could say that this is because the only demand on the child is to be busy in play; experiment could, however, be made in developing a pre-school curriculum which would place greater demands on the child and open up wider fields to him, whilst keeping him happy and absorbed. An important step in such curriculum development would be the statement of very specific goals. Without this step, it is difficult for the teacher to devise a programme to achieve her aims, and even more difficult for the teacher or anyone else to evaluate the extent to which the aims have been achieved. Thus, it is relatively easy to teach reading and measure one's success, much less easy (although not impossible) if the goal is self-confidence or autonomy.

However, there are both organizational and ideological difficulties in attempting to develop a new curriculum in the nursery school. Organizationally, the break in the school system at the age of five means that it is impossible to plan the education of young children as a whole. The age before five, when learning is most rapid, becomes 'pre-school' and not directly related to schooling after five. Ideologically, the nursery school is strongly committed to self-directed play, whilst in the primary school there is a rather abrupt change of emphasis to instructional learning, and the acquisition of decontextualized skills. Research in curriculum development could only occur through very close and ongoing collaboration between research workers and interested teachers. The need for such collaboration was emphasized by many of those interviewed, who deplore the big gap between theory and practice in pre-school education. There is very little application of theory in the pre-school, and people who are concerned with developing ideas about learning, cognitive skills, language and even the educational process rarely spell out the implications of their theories for the practitioner. There is a strong academic tradition in this country which inhibits research workers from plunging into the practical field. Yet those research workers who have attempted to influence educational practice stress that much the most effective method is to work alongside teachers, helping them with problems which they see to be important, and incorporating their knowledge and expertise in the research plan. One of the most important developments needed in this country is more opportunity for teachers to work in a team with psychologists and sociologists. This would not only hopefully enrich the teacher's practice, but provide an opportunity to test the effectiveness of theory.

V
Comments

Joan Tough, Institute of Education, University of Leeds

In undertaking this survey, it was clear from the outset that Barbara Tizard had accepted a difficult task. For research to be planned, so that all the important issues are examined, a review of this kind from time to time becomes essential. The problem is, however, that if such a survey is to be useful it must be made quickly, so that planning can be informed. That Barbara Tizard was able, in a period of three months, to cover so much ground, contacting research workers and documenting so much, is no mean feat.

The review indicates, if nothing more, that early childhood education is now recognized in this country as a proper subject for study and serious research. At the same time, it reflects the difficulties and the general confusion with which those who engage in research in this field will be surrounded.

In carrying out the survey of on-going projects which in any way relate to the education of the young child, Barbara Tizard focuses attention on many aspects, and indicates a range of questions which need to be examined. Those who are presently engaged in planning research in early childhood education will be grateful for this timely indication of the areas in which research is most needed.

In addition to the review of research projects, the opinions of many who have carried out work, or are at present engaged in such work, were collected. Although these were of interest, it may be that this method of reporting tends to reduce the authenticity of the views expressed. Whilst what is reported is undoubtedly part of what was said in interviews, inevitably selection has to be made, and what is selected may not fully represent the consultants' viewpoints. Written statements would perhaps have reflected more nearly the considered opinions of those who gave them.

The third element in the review, Barbara Tizard's own interpretation of what she had uncovered, and the framework in which she examines it, tends to make the report a controversial document for some people. For example, although there is perhaps a problem in knowing quite what 'education' is in early childhood, the term 'pre-school education' for some constitutes a basic contradiction. For those for whom 'education' is a term which is reserved for referring to the institutions through which society intervenes in the life of the individual in order to transmit values, attitudes, skills and knowledge, rejecting the 'narrow definition' creates difficulties. Using this 'narrow definition', 'education' would not include the activities of 'upbringing' which go on within families.

The term 'education' used in this sense refers not only to the processes by which skills and knowledge are transmitted, but also to the development of attitudes, values and qualities of mind by which the individual becomes a viable and acceptable member of the community and, in this country, able to participate in a democratic way of life.

It may be difficult to see what 'education' might offer to the young child which the family might not, but the notion of an 'educated' three-, four- or five-year-old might include moving towards self-control and self-discipline, becoming responsible and reflective, capable of communicating his thinking to others, and having an impetus towards knowing about and understanding the world in which he lives.

That many schools and classes in which education is supposed to be going on fail to produce an 'educated' child is saying something about schools rather than negating the concept of education. That some parents deliberately set out to provide experiences which produce this same development in the child does not destroy the separate notions of 'upbringing' and 'education'. In such cases we can see that 'upbringing' is compatible with 'education'. But it is also clear that in many homes what is offered as 'upbringing' is not at all compatible with what would be seen as 'education'.

The problem arises when we think of all that the child learns in the home as 'education'. The child may learn to be dependent, rather than independent, to be defiant and aggressive, rather than self-controlled and self-disciplined, he may learn not to be curious or interested in the world around him. It does not alter the case to say that children learn to be like this in some schools. Education is a process entrusted to schools: that many schools may not fulfil the aims of education is the strongest argument for curriculum development and change.

To use a wider definition of education on the grounds that there is little to distinguish what almost all mothers are trying to do from what nursery schools set out to do, except by the 'varying degrees of excellence', is not only to impede discussion, but also to make a generalization which seems altogether unjustified.

Many parents may not do any of those activities which can be described as 'educational'. They may not look at books, read stories, sing rhymes, develop a wide range of language skills or help the children to build up a wide general knowledge about the world around them. Indeed, it is frequently argued that it is because many parents do not see such activities as part of their parental role that so many children are at considerable disadvantage when they come to school. This, too, might be too simple a view of the situation.

Even those parents who do see their role as one of 'educating' their children may not succeed in producing an 'educated' child. They may only make him over-anxious, aggressive and demanding, intolerant of other children, hostile to other adults, unable to communicate with others easily, unaware of other people's needs, and lacking in self-control and self-direction.

To have taken a narrower view of education, perhaps, might have led to a closer examnation of what there is in being educated besides learning to read and write, or to develop some concepts and acquire language structures. And this in turn might have provided a framework against which 'educational programmes' and 'educational strategies' might have been viewed. For any test of the effectiveness of programmes should include an assessment, not only of the child's growing knowledge and skill, but also of the development of attitudes towards inquiry and learning which may be crucial aspects of the child's education.

However, even if the wider definition of education used by Barbara Tizard is used, it seems odd to find that a review entitled *Early Childhood Education* has so little to do with children in nursery schools and classes and so little reflection of the opinion of child educators. Amongst the 48 people consulted, only five or six of these had been practitioners in early childhood education or primary education.

This fact is, perhaps, a reflection of the state and status of early childhood education in this country. After decades of neglect, with few teachers being trained for work with young children, a reliance in many areas on nursery nurses for staffing rather than teachers, it is not surprising that there are few who ever enter research. To say that nursery education has 'failed' is to fail to understand the conditions under which nursery schools have operated in the past. Whatever judgements are to be made of the value and effectiveness of nursery education ought to be left until there has been adequate opportunity for reconsidering and redirecting nursery education in the light of new knowledge about young children's growth and learning, and for preparing adequate numbers of teachers who understand the purpose and possibilities of education for the young child.

It is against this background that the research which is looking at nursery education and intervention programmes should be seen. The fact that there has been a growing awareness that early childhood is an important period of development has focused attention on what nursery education might offer to children who come from homes where their early learning is incompatible with, and an inadequate preparation for, what is expected in school. It is this part of the report to which we turn now.

One of the problems of reviewing ongoing research is that the results are not available, and even if they are, they must be set against the background of former research. The danger is that the inferences which are drawn may not justify making statements with any confidence. Where crucial decisions may be taken as a result, there must be the utmost caution exercised whenever statements are made.

In all these studies it is important to consider the methods by which the progress made by children was assessed. Generally, language training is a major feature of the programmes of intervention quoted, for example in the NFER study which uses the Peabody Language Development Kit. The methods of assessment are then tests of language, for example, the Illinois Test of Psycholinguistic Abilities. As a result, a narrow range of skills forms the basis of comparison and many other areas of learning are neglected.

The review treats this area very lightly in discussion. Two British projects are described, and 'numerous American studies' are dismissed in these three words, without any examination of the contents of the programmes used with children, or of the methods of assessment, or of a consideration of what constitutes practice in the traditional nursery schools. Yet these researches are used to draw inferences which might crucially affect decisions that might be taken when policy on setting up nursery schools or classes is being considered.

On the basis of these studies, Barbara Tizard concludes that 'the paucity of projects in this section (the effects of nursery school attendance) probably reflects the fact that most research workers by now consider that the simpler questions about the influence of nursery school attendance on children's achievement have been answered' (p. 00). An alternative inference might be that there are few people around who are qualified to be asking questions about it, and that so far only the most obvious question has been put. There remain numerous questions to be asked about the effectiveness of particular educational strategies, about teacher–child interaction, about the frequency and length of interaction, about teacher–child staffing ratios, about motivation in children's learning, about the effectiveness of teachers in the development of skills and techniques for helping children to learn. We have hardly begun to look at the possibilities, and yet, from the review, the inference is that we know all there is to know about this matter, and with such a degree of confidence, *viz.*, 'In so far, then, as the expansion of early schooling is seen as a way of avoiding later school failure, or of closing the social class gap in achievement, *we already know* it to be doomed to failure. It would perhaps be sensible for research workers to point this out very clearly to public authorities at an early stage' (p. 4).

This is a remarkable statement on the basis of the evidence and so are the assumptions that are made about the thinking behind the expansion of nursery education. There is the implicit assumption that all those who press for such an expansion believe that nursery education *by itself* could have long-term effects on children's achievement, regardless of what follows later; or that *by itself* nursery education could close the social gap. This is to infer a degree of naivety which is quite unjustified. Those who want to bring about changes in this direction are likely to recognize the whole range of changes that need to be brought about; for example, through the education of parents about ways of bringing up children and by informing the potential parent whilst still at school about the importance of experiences in early childhood and on matters of child care. At the same time, they are likely to be arguing the importance of bringing about changes, both in primary and secondary schools, which would increase the possibilities for disadvantaged children to gain more from their time in school. They are likely also to be pressing for changes to be brought about in the social conditions in which many children are brought up.

It would indeed be naive to think that the effects of two years of nursery education, even when 'effective educational strategies' have been developed, could withstand ten or eleven years in schools that fail to recognize and meet the problem. But who indeed ever thought that this was so? Certainly none of the researchers that were consulted in this survey.

Can nursery education contribute anything in the task of breaking the cycle of disadvantage? There is much more research yet to be done before that question can be answered. In the meantime, there is no doubt that children and mothers benefit from nursery education in the short term and that in itself might be worth something.

The review certainly provides us with a much needed view of what is going on in this country. The main inference must surely be how much more is needed.

PRE-SCHOOL AND/OR EDUCATION: A COMMENT

Marion Blank, New Jersey College of Medicine and Dentistry, Rutgers Medical School

Dr Tizard has covered so many complex and important issues in her monograph that it is well nigh impossible, in a short comment, to do justice to the total range of ideas that were mentioned. Accordingly, I would like to limit my comments to highlighting and expanding upon a theme that was subtly but nevertheless clearly present throughout the paper. Specifically, I am referring to the two major, but separate, forces responsible for the expansion of pre-school services. One force stems from the desire of women to have support services in the rearing of their children; the other derives from the use of pre-schools as a possible means of preventing future academic failure. For purposes of simplifying communication, I will henceforth refer to the former as 'shared rearing pre-schools' and to the latter as 'academic pre-schools'· There are, of course, a number of points of convergence between these two types of pre-schools, e.g. the use of materials that are attractive to children; the possible provision of preventative medical services, etc. Nevertheless, I believe these forces, and the structures they lead to, are so different that any attempt to merge them at this time will only obscure already complex and controversial issues.

The general failure to separate forces as diverse as these is by no means unique to the pre-school situation. It is characteristic of almost any analysis relating to children. For example, the fields of both psychology and education typically group children, and those who work with children, along the parameter of age rather than topic. Thus, in psychology, no one will think it is at all unusual to hear a professional refer to himself as a 'child psychologist'. But many an eyebrow would be raised if a comparable professional referred to himself as an 'adult psychologist'. Rather than using the dimension of age, the person concerned with adult functioning defines himself according to a problem area so that his self-description is in such terms as 'clinical psychologist', 'neuropsychologist', and 'industrial psychologist'. Many of these divisions are applicable to the study of children and therefore a person interested in children could easily define himself in these terms. But he, or she, rarely does so.

It is this failure to differentiate that has led us all too easily to consider the variety of pre-school services as a single entity. Just because the same age-range children are involved, however, it does not mean that the same issues or problems are present. It is as if we decided to combine a factory and a university together under the name 'adult activity centre' simply because they both contain persons over 18 years of age for prolonged stretches of time during traditional working hours. There are points of similarity between the two institutions and a case could be made for the unification. Nevertheless, in exclusively focusing on the similarity, a great deal of information is lost about crucial differences. I believe a similar point holds for the two types of pre-school education. In emphasizing this point, I do not wish to imply that the study of the child will be enhanced if the child is 'dissected' into as many subparts as possible. Rather, I believe that the care of 'the whole child' in any setting will be much more effective if, beforehand, one has analysed the uniqueness of the situation as fully as possible.

The differences between the two pre-school forces are evident in almost any aspects of the problem that one might wish to consider. This includes the question of goals, curriculum, the role of the teacher, methods of evaluation, structure and timing of the instruction, and the role of experimental findings. In order to gain a clearer picture of the differences it seems valuable to consider briefly each of these points relative to the two pre-school forces. First I will consider the 'shared rearing pre-school' which, as noted above, is designed to provide the parents of young children with services to aid them in the responsibilities of child care. As such, the major purpose of programmes within the framework is to offer a service that will help the parents and the entire family to function in a more effective and more enjoyable manner. I believe this goal to be of inestimable value. Frequently, however, it is not recognized as such. In part, the lack of recognition may stem from the fact that this sort of service is seen primarily as a support to mothers. Accordingly, as with so many other issues concerning the needs of women, it has not been awarded a high priority by society. All those familiar with the extraordinary amount of care required by young children will, however, recognize the crucial help that such a service can provide to the people in question.

There are, however, other forces which have led us to neglect the value of 'shared rearing pre-schools'. We live in a society that places tremendous value on formal education while simultaneously rarely considering the support of widespread services to enhance the ease of living. As a result any group requesting support, in particular, government support, for the expansion of 'shared rearing' services will downplay the ease aspect and emphasize the educational aspect in the hope that the picture so drawn will make the programmes more attractive. (Given that the bulk of my experience has been in the United States, my comments may be more valid for that situation. Nevertheless, my observations in other technologically advanced nations lead me to think that similar conditions pertain in many other countries as well.) The political wisdom of an approach which upgrades 'education' and downplays 'shared rearing' remains to be determined, i.e. perhaps it may lead to more readily obtaining support for pre-school programmes. But it seems clear that this approach has also been a factor in forcing 'shared rearing pre-schools' to take on educational purposes which they were never intended to serve and which they may well not be suited to fulfill.

An acknowledgement of 'shared rearing' as the key function of one type of pre-school in no way lessens the complexities of what must be known to design and operate an effective pre-school. But the 'priorities' are quite different from that commonly associated with the word 'school'. The major goal now is not to change, educate, alter or modify the child along particular lines, although this may occur. Rather it is to provide, during the hours of the day when the children are in the schools, a secure benign environment that is compatible with the interests and predispositions of the young child. This somewhat 'indirect' provision of services is by no means unique to the 'shared rearing pre-school'. For instance, the primary function of a hospital is not to feed people. However, given the needs of the human organism, it is sensible and desirable to offer them food as nutritious as possible during their stay.

The provision of a humane and interesting environment for young children might have been a problem some generations back—before the work of pioneers such as Montessori, Froebel and Dewey. Even now, our care of children can be improved in many areas, e.g. more flexible hours not so tightly tied to the working day; centres closer to the children's homes, etc. Nevertheless, it seems clear that with our present knowledge—and adequate funding—one could provide an appealing, supportive environment for most young children if one chose to do so—and if the parents wanted them to be in such a setting.

Given these loose constraints and the great adaptability of the human organism, the actual structure of any programme in a 'shared rearing pre-school' could vary considerably. For example, major dimension of variability might be the degree of structured activity, i.e. some programmes could be quite structured, others could consist much more of free-play. Regardless of the variability in the programmes, however, the role of the 'curriculum' would be minimal—if one uses the term 'curriculum' according to the common meaning of offering a body of knowledge and information to the learner that would not readily be available in his usual environment. The issue will perhaps become clearer if we examine it with reference to the measurable effects of having attended school. Thus, we can say with a reasonable degree of assurance that the average child is much less likely to be literate if he does not have some sort of formal schooling. In that sense, failure to experience the curricula of formal education will have marked and measureable effects on the child's functioning. One would be hard-pressed, however, to identify a comparable set of skills that would fail to emerge if the child did not attend pre-school. In this sense, failure to be exposed to the 'curricula' of pre-school education will not have the same sort of measurable effects on his behaviour. In this context, if one wished to retain the term 'curriculum' for the pre-school then it would seem most appropriate to have it take on the meaning of making available to the child materials that are appealing so that he may employ or rehearse his skills—skills that he is acquiring at a particular age regardless of whether he is in a 'shared rearing school' or not.

Pursuit of this line of reasoning leads one to conclude that the training of teachers for this setting would not focus on curriculum transmission, but on the observation of normal behaviour, on understanding the breadth and limitations of young children's skills, on dealing with the needs and concerns of parents, and most important, on understanding the dynamics of group interaction and on developing ways to effect good interchange among members of a group. With the exception of the family and group dynamic emphasis, the current training of most pre-school personnel is well suited to the demands they will meet in the work situation.

Methods of evaluating 'shared rearing pre-school' programmes also do not seem to pose insuperable problems. It seems reasonable to ask that the evaluation focus on the goals of the programme, namely, on the provision of services to ease the burdens on the parents. Therefore, if the parents were pleased and if the children were content, then such a programme would, and should, be considered successful.

Once established, 'shared rearing pre-schools' could function not only as a service to the families involved. They could also be valuable centres for research on young children's behaviour and on the types of organizations most suitable for encouraging healthy development in children. In this context, many of the suggestions raised by the investigators interviewed by Dr Tizard could serve as catalysts for research. In particular, studies could be carried out on children's interests in art and music, children's spontaneous use of language with adults and peers, the optimal physical organization of a room, etc. Such research findings could then provide the basis for improving the 'shared rearing pre-school' centres. But the establishment and expansion of such centres need not wait for these research findings. Enough expertise is currently available to set up reasonably effective centres at present if society sees this as a valuable goal.

The question of 'academic pre-schools' presents a totally different picture. Here the central goal is not day care, but education. As such these programmes belong not to the area of the pre-school age *per se*, but to the area of specialized education which runs the gamut of ages—from pre-school to university level. Perhaps the major difference between 'academic pre-schools' and other specialized educational efforts is that the educational demands placed on the former are so extensive as to go beyond the demands placed upon any other educational unit. For example, in other areas of schooling, as noted above, the academic goal is to transmit a curriculum covering a limited and specified subject matter, e.g. a particular section of mathematics, a beginning set of reading skills, a section of European history, etc. The goal of the 'academic pre-school', however, is not the transmission of a limited subject matter. Rather it is a basic alteration in the child's level of functioning so that not only all present academic learning, but all future academic learning will be enhanced. It is only such an ambitious goal that allows one to conclude that a programme has 'failed'—not because it has failed to achieve immediate gains, but because the gains were not sustained after the children left the programme. It is probably also such an ambitious goal that has focused us almost exclusively on the maintenance of gains and has led us to ignore other, equally important, issues. For instance, one rarely hears the question of whether specialized programmes can be initiated as effectively at later ages if there have been no special efforts to foster change when the child was in an earlier stage of development. In asking this question, the criterion of success of an 'academic pre-school' becomes not 'self-maintenance of gain', but rather the school's role in permitting the child to remain open to later specialized instruction if and when it is made available to him.

Regardless of the criterion of success, it may well prove to be the case that the goals of an 'academic pre-school' are unattainable, in that excessive and unique demands have been placed upon this type of educational unit. But equally, it must be said that our efforts until now have hardly been of a nature sufficient to yield a definite answer to the problem. In fact, partly because of the failure to differentiate between 'shared rearing' and 'academic pre-schools', many initial efforts at the latter were merely the implementation of the former with the exception that the population involved mainly children from lower socio-economic backgrounds. Given the fact that 'shared rearing' programmes were not designed with educational goals in the forefront, it is not surprising that such programmes often failed to achieve the hoped-for change.

With the problem formulated in this manner, it seems evident that such issues as curriculum, evaluation, and implementation take on a radically different colouring than they did for the 'shared rearing' programmes. First of all, the curriculum and its method of presentation become crucial. The issue now is no longer one of solely presenting material that is age-appropriate and appealing. Instead, the material becomes the chief source for effecting basic changes in the way the child deals with demands related to the academic setting. Co-existing with this increase in demand for precise curricula is the rather dismaying absence of information necessary for the design of such curricula. Instead, the field is strewn with controversy and confusion. For example as Dr Tizard's report indicates, there is evidence from a variety of sources that the area of language may be a particularly crucial one for children who are likely to experience difficulty at school. However, the issue of what, if anything, needs changing is hotly debated as we have all witnessed in the well known 'difference-deficit' controversy (see Bernstein, 1972; Ginsburg, 1972; Labov, 1970.)

It may be instructive at this point to elaborate somewhat on the gap between what is known from the experimental laboratory and what is needed for the teaching situation. Because my own work has been in the area of language, I will use this area to illustrate the points I wish to make. However, comparable difficulties hold for other areas relevant to the development of effective 'academic pre-school' programmes, i.e. motivation, attention, etc. Specifically, for many years in the area of language research, words were viewed primarily as a tool in concept formation, e.g. through the use of a word such as *animal*, it was felt that we could meaningfully group, in a single category, such diverse creatures as a snail, elephant and sparrow. Language in its other roles, in particular in its role as a means of communication, was barely touched upon. In other words, language was seen almost exclusively as a skill *within* a person, and not as a medium of exchange *between* persons. The absence of techniques and models from the latter perspective is particularly crucial for the school, for it represents a situation that relies heavily upon linguistic interchange for both assessing and altering a child's functioning.

Once the communication aspects of language are fully recongized it may well help us broaden our understanding of the school situation. For example, at the outset of the monograph, Dr Tizard states that 'the curriculum of the nursery school can hardly be distinguished from that of the home' (p. viii). As long as the study of language is confined to units such as words and sentences uttered by a single person, then this generalization appears to have validity. For example, a mother at home might well say, 'Oh it's nearly time to go. Let's put these things away', and a teacher in school might say the same thing. Similarly a child at home and at school could easily be heard to utter nearly identical statements in the two settings. Once the linguistic analysis goes beyond the sentence uttered by one person and considers the communication network, the picture changes considerably. Then the crucial measure is not the type of sentence, but such measures as 'who initiated the exchange?', 'over how many interchanges was the exchange maintained?', and 'how relevant was the utterance to the content and to what the other person just said or did?'. As the communication functions of language have become to be recognized, work has begun to grow in interactional analyses of language behaviour (Allen, 1973; Olson, 1974; Sinclair and Coulthard, 1974). As it develops further, I believe that it will show that there are dramatic differences between the language of the home and of the pre-school class.

Even if such data are obtained, however, they will not automatically offer ways in which the language of the classroom can be made to be more like the language of the home (even if that is a desirable goal). In addition, such data will not automatically offer a solution to the problem of how to facilitate productive exchanges in children who enter the school with limited mastery in this sphere (Tough, 1973). In this connection, it is unimportant whether the behaviour that one wishes to foster is in the sphere of language, of perception, or attention or motivation. Regardless of the area, the same problem holds: specific-ally, the documentation of the normative acquisition of a skill by no means indicates the method that must be employed to foster those skills in children who are experiencing difficulty. For example, as Dr Tizard points out on pages 9 and 63, the children most in need of attention usually are the ones least likely to receive such attention. I do not believe that this state of affairs stems from lack of awareness or prejudice on the part of the teacher. Rather, it seems to reflect the fact that most people feel more comfortable in speaking with others who speak freely in return and, conversely, feel less comfortable in speaking with others who are likely to be taciturn. A resolution to this problem will not come from simply telling teachers to 'speak more' because as any smoker knows, people do not readily change long-ingrained dis-positions by a simple statement that they should do so. Instead, if a solution is to be found, it will depend upon the development of well-delineated techniques that will enable a teacher to overcome the obstacles inherent in this type of exchange.

From this vantage point, it seems clear that the problem of teacher education in an 'academic pre-school' is very different from that for a 'shared rearing pre-school'. The teachers' role must go beyond that of providing an effective, pleasant environment in which to live. Instead, they must structure the material, information, and language in extremely precise ways if they are to achieve the ambitious goal of altering the children's manner of functioning in the entire academic sphere (see Blank, 1973; and Frankenstein, 1972, for illustrations of the type of care that the teacher must exert). Needless to say, the burden on the teacher in such a setting is much greater than it has been until now and furthermore the information necessary to enable the teacher to cope with such demands is not as yet even available.

As a result of all these factors, in contrast to 'shared rearing' programmes, 'academic pre-school' programmes cannot at present be meaningfully initiated on a large scale. This is not to say that no programmes should be initiated. Rather, I believe it essential that the programmes be initiated on a small, carefully controlled scale which can answer specific questions, such as: 'What material and interchange is most effective in altering specific behaviours?' 'At what age is it easiest to effect changes?' 'How should the group be organized to obtain maximal gains?' 'Should parents be trained?' If so, 'should their training be directed to getting them to serve as "teachers" to their own children?'. It seems that only through projects directed at questions such as these will we be able to gradually piece together the information needed, if we are to know whether effective 'academic pre-school' programmes can be established. The investment, however, is more in terms of a long-term commitment in time and involvement rather than in massive infusions of money for short periods of time. The absence of ready solutions at the moment, moreover, should not serve as a major deterrent to work in this area, for the problems are not unique to the 'academic pre-school'. Many of the central problems in our society —for example, the treatment of the aged—require a similar long-term commitment with no immediate pay-off necessarily forthcoming. I believe that should we fail to make the effort to reach and help members of our community, society will be far poorer for all its citizens.

References

ALLEN, D. (1973) *The development of prediction in child language.* Unpublished doctoral dissertation. New York: Teachers College Columbia University.

BERNSTEIN, B. (1972) *Class, Codes and control.* London: Routledge and Kegan Paul.

BLANK, M. (1973) *Teaching learning in the pre-school: A dialogue approach.* Columbus, Ohio: Charles Merrill.

FRANKENSTEIN, C. (1972) *They think again: Summary of an educational experiment with disadvantaged adolescents.* Jerusalem, Israel: Report from the School of Education, Hebrew University.

GINSBURG, H. (1972) *The myth of the deprived child.* Englewood Cliffs, New Jersey: Prentice Hall.

Comments *103*

LABOV, W. (1970) *The logic of non-standard English in Language and Poverty*. Ed. F. Williams. Chicago: Markham.

OLSON, D. R. (1974) *From utterance to text: The bias of language in speech and writing*. Paper presented at the Epistemics meeting. Nashville, Tenn.: Vanderbilt University.

SINCLAIR, J. and COULTHARD, R. M. (1975) *Towards an analysis of discourse: The English used by teachers and pupils*. London: Oxford University Press.

TOUGH, J. (1973) *The language of young children in education, in the early years*. Ed. M. Chazan. University College of Swansea. Aberfan Disaster Fund.

DOING RESEARCH THAT MIGHT MAKE A DIFFERENCE

Jerome Bruner, Oxford University

I

The concluding section of Dr Tizard's report concerns itself with 'general issues', prominent among which is 'The communication and implementation of research findings'. It is plain from her summary of conversations with research workers that they are unhappy about the state of affairs that now prevails. But as one reads on, it soon becomes apparent that the problem is not so much a matter of communicating or implementing research findings, however imperfect those processes may be, but rather goes much deeper into the very nature of much of our 'applied research'. The trouble appears to be with the research process itself, its separateness from the concerns of those who would use specialized knowledge to guide their conduct of affairs. The more thoughtful among her respondents remark on the fact that too often the very nature of the research is remote from the concerns of the practitioner, let alone the difficulty of communicating it and interpreting it.

This remoteness is worrisome on several scores. In the first place, it persists in spite of the fact that many research workers who devote themselves to clarifying issues involved in the decent conduct of human societies begin with the highest ideals and with a strong will to better whatever the situation is to which they are directing their efforts. The failure is not for lack of trying. Nor, in the second place, can it be said that practitioners are unwilling to accept help either in the form of better information or recommendations for better practice. Doubtless there are 'resistances' to new ideas, but this could surely not be the whole of the story. Moreover, I find it difficult to believe that the issue is a matter of media—an absence of journals or reviews prepared to disseminate crucial ideas about the conduct of education or, to bring it down to the matter at hand, the conduct of pre-school education. The magazines and reviews, to be sure, are not in profusion (though they probably would be if there were matters of great moment to communicate and debate), nor is the readership particularly large or keen (but that again is not all to be laid to laziness either). Nor can I find it in myself to put the blame on the dullness of pedagogical writing which, I think, is an effect of deeper causes rather than being itself the cause of the remoteness that prevails between applied educational research and the practice to which it is supposed to relate. Besides, engineering research which *is* heeded by practitioners is hardly inspired by muses! Finally, I would urge that we should not look for explanation to deep historical or political forces, tempting though it may be to do so. Doubtless there are such, not the least of them being that the practice of education is a reflection of a society's political aspirations. The issue of comprehensive schools *versus* some other mode of grouping students is by no means exclusively to be resolved by finding out which technique of grouping produces the most literate or numerate population nor even which produces the most democratic feelings in the population of the next generation. But even politically determined decisions can be affected, enlivened, and rendered more humane by an input of useful knowledge about their consequences. The demise of the Eleven-plus examination was surely hastened by some timely research by Himmelweit and Swift indicating that it was *not* achieving the objective of equalizing opportunity by rewarding merit.

The deep problem, I think, inheres in the use of research in human situations generally—whether education, marriage, work, or worship. It stems from the profoundly subtle task of generating knowledge that in a general sense is useful but which, at the same time, is seen by those who must use it as not only useful but relevant to them and to their own conduct of the enterprise. It is often said that this difficulty arises from the absence of a clear-cut criterion by which we may judge whether a notion or some particular knowledge is relevant to some human practice. The health sciences, we hear, have much less difficulty because it is clear when one is healthy or sick, alive or dead, and one can easily tell whether some proposed practice or remedy will move us from one to the other side of such dichotomies. But while the clarity of criterion surely matters, it surely cannot be the whole story, else Lake Erie would not have become a dead sea nor cigarette smoking have increased since the Surgeon General's and the Royal College of Physician's Reports.

Finally, before turning to the main enterprise, we must dispose of one nagging suspicion, that the reason why we do not use research much to guide our practice in raising and educating the young is that the research has nothing much to tell us that would be of much use. Or to put it in a more kindly light, what research on development, learning, socialization, etc., has to tell us is so complicated and contingent on conditions prevailing at the time of their application, that it is of little avail compared with other, unforeseeable forces. The unkindly version of this suspicion is plainly silly. A very great deal is known about human learning and memory, about attention and perception, about the effects of stress and some of the conditions that produce it, and so on. *Not* a great deal of it is wildly counter-intuitive and alien from common sense (though some of it is), but a great deal of it is applicable to the way we teach, the way we encourage children to play, the nature of the 'lessons' we organize, and so on. The memory performance of educationally subnormal children can be hugely improved by giving them some training in 'reworking' matters to be remembered, even to the point that it is virtually indistinguishable from 'normal' memory—to take one matter at random from research of the last few years. Yet we don't use the finding in school practice, nor for that matter do we ever think about memory strategies as a fit subject for children's games.

So we must examine the more kindly version of the suspicion—we know things, yes, but they are so contingent on so many other things that they are virtually impossible to use. And that leads me to the exercise that is the main point of this paper. How do we make knowledge useful, even if the knowledge is not the most powerful, and even if the situations in which it is to be applied are full of unexpected pitfalls? What I wish to examine is how one organizes research related to improving human practice in human situations in the absence of highly reliable criteria of relevance.

II

Let me begin by distinguishing between troubles, problems, and puzzles. A trouble is a difficulty so ill-defined as to seem incapable of alleviation. A puzzle is a difficulty, on the other hand, that is so *well* defined as to permit of a unique solution or at least of a class of determinate solutions, as in chess which is a colligation of puzzles that change with the situation on the board. Scientific models or theories are among the most interesting and useful puzzle forms ever developed by man, and now that we are able to design aids for their construction and resolution—computing devices—they are becoming more so. Finally, a problem is constructed when a puzzle form is successfully imposed upon a trouble to render it potentially solvable. Now, in the world as it exists, the presenting symptoms of a social issue or an educational issue, is usually in the form of a trouble. 'The trouble with pre-schools is that they do not . . .' and the final phrase usually specifies some capacity that is to be improved. In that same world, where there is research and theory-making, one finds people who are building puzzle forms that they think have particular utility for rendering such troubles into solvable problems. The task, put in these terms, is to find a way of getting the two parties together, and we shall approach it in the same spirit as we have urged that sensible men approach all such problems. If it can be done as elegantly as the solution of getting the cannibals and missionaries across the river, that will be splendid. Alas we cannot. So how to proceed?

The first principle of a solution is to find out what in fact the two sides do—those who locate or simply experience trouble, and those who manufacture models and theories. There is little that need be said about the first group. A trouble is a given in any system. What then of the researcher who thinks of himself as attempting to create models that might shed light on educational deprivation, crime, illiteracy, indiscipline, etc.? Inevitably, model- or theory-making proceeds with principal regard to the virtues of simplicity and generality, the two virtues that indeed endow theory-building with its uniqueness. For a theory is a canny way of taking account of a great deal of complexity whilst actually keeping very little in mind, and it achieves this astonishing result precisely by reducing variation to its underlying invariance. The rewards within the research community are for generality and for elegant simplicity. And, of course, these hallmarks are in an ancient sense the proper ones for the products of the creator of fruitful models. Such models do in fact 'fit' the phenomena of physical and biological nature they were designed to account for.

But there are three difficulties that beset this process of model-building in those human sciences that deal with such matters as the raising of the young, the conduct of human relationships, and indeed, even the management of economic affairs. The first relates to the procedure for assuring 'fit.' In the natural sciences, the canonical procedure is to find paradigm cases which one uses for experiment. To study the nervous system, for example, one takes an idealized segment of nervous system activity—like single nerve-fibre transmission—and submits it to exhaustive experimental observation, hoping to build a proper model for the myriad results that find their way into 'the literature'. There emerges something akin to a Dutch tulip craze: all the bright young men come on board, and soon there begins to emerge a 'reality' that is dominated by a theory—say, in this case, the theory of nerve transmission as a wave of disturbance travelling down a monomolecular film—and by a procedure—the single nerve fibre preparation studied electrochemically. The domination of such paradigms has been well described by Thomas Kuhn in his shrewd book on *The Structure of Scientific Revolution*. When paradigms become established, science ceases to consider phenomena as these are en-countered in the everyday world and begins to concentrate on more selected phenomenon or narrow ranges of phenomena. To the degree that a science has a connected map of its own terrain, the canonical procedure plainly pays off, for each paradigmatic piece fits into a broader view of nature. But where a science does *not* have such a map, it becomes 'phenomena ridden'. My own science of psychology is a striking case in point, and if one takes the instance of 'learning theory', the shortcoming is glaring. For what has emerged from a half-century of research is a series of rather unconnected (and often successively deserted) intensely studied, isolated phenomena of interest principally to those who have been engaged in investigating them—reinforcement schedules, the law of emphasis, discrimination learning, the conditions for Pavlovian conditioning such as the interval between conditioned stimulus (CS) and unconditioned stimulus (US), etc., etc. Though courses for teachers often use textbooks that devote a chapter or two to recounting the results of such paradigmatic exercises, it is highly questionable (and often questioned) whether they contribute anything at all to the teacher's understanding of learning as it is to be observed in school—or, for that matter, out of school! This is not to say that research on learning did not start with a genuine impulse to help in the practical world, for it can be demonstrated historically that it did (see for example, G. W. Allport's account of the theory of identical elements in his *Personality*). Rather, what happens is that the paradigm takes over: 'the literature' rather than phenomena as encountered increasingly sets the researchable problem.

The second besetting difficulty is the separation that then comes to exist between the practitioner concerned with aiding learning *in vivo*—teacher, curriculum maker, remedialist, and the like—and the investigator of 'literature' phenomena *in vitro*. Their institutional affiliations become separated: they teach in different departments, go to different meetings, achieve their rewards for different deeds, even very likely develop different character structures. Indeed, even when 'reform movements' develop on the 'model maker's' side, as with the emergence of cognitive psychology as an antidote to the barrenness of learning theory, the forces are such as to lead it down the same garden path, as witness a recent review article by Alan Allport (*Quart. J. Exp. Psychol.*, Feb. 1975) in which he examines the last decade of research in this promising field and laments that it too has gone the way of chasing 'literature' phenomena with little accumulation of a connected view of the processes by which men come to know their environments. In sum, a strong cultural division develops that seems to fix the two approaches—practice and research—into institutionalized amber.

The third besetting difficulty is the emergence of a new kind of research community closely connected with the practitioner, engaged in grinding out 'practically' orientated data that lack generality and elegance and in their interpretability throw, at best, dim light on some particular problem. I do not mean to be harsh on educational research, at least no harsher than I have been on psychological research, but it is hard to make a case for the utility of some of the number-crunching efforts that have been designed to evaluate how well the practitioner's efforts have come off.

In the end, the practitioner, given little aid in his struggles with trouble, develops his own fashions in explanation: theories of education, theories of child rearing, theories of genetic endowment, theories about the deprived child, and the rest. And interestingly enough, these become matters of public debate, often fierce public debate. Not only is Dr Spock accused of having 'softened' a generation of the young with his 'theories' of child rearing, but even Dr Spock comes to believe that his theories may have done just that, and he publicly recants! What is interesting about such 'theories' is that they *may* be right or they *may* be wrong. They are so stated, alas, that one would never be able to find out. Nonetheless, they develop a cultural reality that may be impressive enough as to have an effect in their own right. Who knows?

Dr Spock *may* have affected a generation, for good or for ill. Whatever the nature of his 'theory' it *did* have an effect on public policy.

In a word, it seems as if the process of designing models for converting troubles into workable problems, is not working very well, if at all. Where do we go from here?

III

I should like to suggest that what is needed is a reformulation of the research process when the research in question is mounted for the alleviation of the kinds of practical social 'troubles' we have been discussing. It is not intended that the proposal be interpreted to include more than that, and certainly not that it should supercede most academic research now done along the lines briefly sketched above. My concern, rather, is with research whose results are to be *applied* in a public setting to social issues.

The central element in the proposal is the definition of the research process itself. Its first feature should be *openness*. From the first, it must be open to discussion in terms of its formulation and design, its eventual policy objectives, and the repercussion of its findings on practice. I like Brian Jackson's term, 'open research,' as a characterization. A first practical step toward formulating such research is to bring together in a team a combination of skills that will assure a healthy exchange of views about the dimensions of the trouble being considered, the nature of the feasible alternatives seen as available options for action, and all of the constraining factors that are foreseeable operative in implementing a solution. All of these must be looked at first from the point of view of the 'phenomenology' of the practitioner and of those who are affected by his practice. Before there can be any move toward reformulating the problem in terms of research, there must be a first step of locating the trouble as experienced by the participants in it. This, in itself, requires a research effort, if only a 'naturalistic' one of observing and discussing and even debating. If we are speaking of schools or of pre-school provisions, then the first step must be to get a direct sense of what the difficulties appear to be from the point of view of teachers, parents, children, local authorities, and so on. I and some colleagues were involved in carrying out research to determine sources of psychological stress operating on submariners in prolonged underwater operations, and it was the genius of that extraordinary service, the US Navy Submarine Service, that they suggested we team up with the crew of the USS *Halfbeak* on a cruise before getting down to it. How else could we have found out about the importance of all members of the crew being seen by all others as having a continuing function (unlike the pharmacist's mate who came into action only when, obviously rarely, a member of the young crew reported on sick call), or that an 'indefinite personality' had somehow to be given a more 'definite one', or that the commander's role by its definition 'felt' isolated and lonely. The theories of claustrophobic anxiety, our model brought with us in our seabags to the dock in New London, Connecticut, died rather hard, even when a chief petty officer told us he loved submarines because it was 'like living inside a watch'! By the end of the study, *we* were submariners, not only in the sense of having done the obligatory tank ascent in a Mommsen Lung, but in having boozed our share in the Underseas Warfare Club and helped design a fantasy submarine called the USS *Tension Release*! All of this occurred because the group of us on the research side were quite properly believed not to know anything about what troubles were like in a highly technical vessel manned by a highly trained crew operating below the surface of the ocean. We began suspicious and suspected, quite rightly. In the end, many of the best researched suggestions directed to the Bureau of Ships for technical changes and to the Bureau of Personnel for changes in organization were joint products of the practitioners and the researchers. In educational research, alas, one begins suspicious and suspected, but it is assumed that both sides *know* what it feels like to the participants in the educational process—after all, we were all educated!

The second step is the formulation of a model, as explicitly as it is possible to do so and with an accounting from all sides as to why or why not the model fits the trouble. Inevitably, this includes the data gathering procedures dictated by the model that are to be employed, and here is one point at which it may well become necessary to carry out pilot research not only to establish feasibility, but to give all parties a sense of how the research procedure meshes with the concerns that initiated the study.

I should like now to make a rather more radical suggestion about the research team—that it include a highly trained, properly specialized journalist who will not only participate in the planning, but also report upon the nature of the debate that it generates. For if the results of the research are to affect the public or some segment of it, and if they are to be implemented by a local education authority or other responsible local bodies, then the openness of the research must extend to them.

Moreover, one can reasonably argue that for results to be comprehensible and for them to be trusted, one must make public the processes by which they were generated. Research on education, at whatever level, is not push-button, its process of formulation being anything but crystal clear. Of particular importance is the need to make plain the relationship between the 'phenomenology' of the trouble as experienced by participants in the social process being studied, and the nature of the research. It is even conceivable that the discussion generated could be of considerable interest not only to readers of a flysheet prepared for local consumption, but also by those who follow such matters generally —in the pages of *The Times Educational Supplement, The Economist, New Society,* as well as in the occasional report by education correspondents in the National Press. Let it be clear that I am not proposing Public Relations, but an airing of the issues concerning how we attempt to solve educational problems.

It follows as a corollary from this that it does not suffice to bury the results of research on public issues in the pages of prestigious learned journals (thereby earning kudos for the researcher), nor to issue them in the heavily insulated prose of Official Reports (in recognition of the practitioners official family). This too requires an openness of approach that is rarely found in modern practice. Indeed, an example of good practice comes to hand readily: Virginia Makins' condensation and reworking of the Bullock Report for the *TES*. If it seems, indeed, that I am proposing a campaign of 'consciousness raising' about research on modern social problems, including education, I will cheerfully confess.

I believe that the process I have described is feasible for several reasons. In the first place, the apparatus of theory and research in the human sciences related to practice is not so technical as to be out of reach of the intelligent layman. There are aspects of it that are more difficult than that, but in the interest of openness they too can be explicated. The Cloze procedure in the teaching of reading noted in the Bullock Report—replacing missing letters with asterisks which the student must fill in in order to read—is based on some interesting, theoretical formations on the role of redundancy. It would be a pity if one felt the Cloze test to be an interesting procedure, *not* to make clear its basis in modern theories and research on information and its relation to coding processes such matters can be made clearer.

George Miller, in his Presidential Address to the American Psychological Association some years ago, proposed that Psychology be given away to the public rather than being channelled through a technological elite concerned with the 'management of men'. It is much in the same spirit that I propose that not only be there instituted a process of open research involving practitioners and research scientists, but also that the process itself be more fully reported to those who will be affected by its outcome.

IV

Who shall initiate such a pattern of 'open research' as here proposed? In Britain, there are three major sources of public research, controlled respectively by the Universities, by the Government and its Ministries, and by the Research Councils. The first two represent, respectively, the researchers and the practitioners. It is to the Research Councils that such an initiative properly falls—operating as honest brokers between the University Research community and those, at whatever level, who deal with the kinds of 'social troubles' that might benefit by translation into more theoretically formulated 'problems'. But obviously the Research Councils have no coercive power, nor should they, save in specifying areas that are candidates for such treatment as we are here proposing, and by taking the first steps toward bringing the partners together. This, indeed, might be conceived as their doing their part for the Roschild 'fraction'.

Surely one of the ways in which the Councils can proceed is precisely by giving their support to groups that are hoping to break new ground in this general direction. In the matter of the present Report—the special problem of pre-school provision for children victimized by social and economic disadvantage—the proper step would be to establish a working seminar that would review critically some of the major presuppositions of those charged with the practice of caring for the pre-school young, as well as the principal models proposed for 'explaining' the effects of poverty and disadvantage on the young— theories of language use, theories of implicit pedagogy, theories of the 'culture of poverty' and its transmission. The object of the exercise would be to design research where needed and to design proposals for intervention where possible, with a view to determining from attempted intervention what in fact operates in real-life contexts when programmes are attempted. Not the least of its functions would be to determine how the trouble looks to those involved in it. In short, it seems to me that a first step is to create the kind of team we have been discussing in the preceding pages, including the elements of public accounting and public reporting. There has already been so much poorly conceived information on the less advantaged young reported in the Press and, indeed, in political debate, that a new start toward open research seems plainly in order.

PRE-SCHOOL RESEARCH: DIRECTIONS AND ORGANIZATION

A. H. Halsey, Nuffield College, Oxford

Dr Barbara Tizard has produced a much-needed, authoritative and comprehensive review of the present state of research on education in early childhood in Great Britain. My intention in commenting on her monograph is certainly not to bury it, nor also merely to praise it for its undoubted merits, but to emphasize and support some of the lessons it offers for the development of research and policy. Dr Tizard's aim was to inform future decisions by the SSRC with respect to the funding of further research. At the same time, since happily or un-happily research theories and findings are related (though in no simple inferential sequence) to policy decisions, she was led to make a number of suggestions and recommendations concerning the provision of pre-school services. She has offered guidance, in short, to both the directions of research and its organization *vis-á-vis* policy and practice.

My comments are intended to supplement these same two purposes. With respect to the research issues, such disciplinary claims as I might have to do so are those of a sociologist rather than a psychologist. With respect to the policy issues, the most immediately relevant experience on which I can draw is that of the EPA research programme in which, as is well known, a good deal of attention was paid to pre-schooling, though the principal focus was on primary schools and the projects included work on relations between homes and schools, remedial teaching, teaching materials and curricula relevant to the experience of EPA children, the training and recompense of teachers in EPA schools, and the synthesis of several of these ideas in the development of the community school.

The EPA programme lay largely, therefore, outside Dr Tizard's purview and her formal terms of reference in any case excluded it since she was asked to review current research on children under five. She did, however, include some brief reference to the pre-school element in the EPA programme because of its impact on subsequent developments. Her judgement was that 'as a result of the EPA programme educational authorities were led to reconsider the adequacy of their provisions for the under-fives, nursery school teachers entered a debate which still continues about the adequacy of their traditional teaching methods, and research workers were led to reconsider the impact which early schooling on its own could have on children's achievements'. I will return to the last of these matters below, but first a more general appraisal of the research situation in this field needs to be made.

The Research task

Dr Tizard's conception of the scope of problems bearing on pre-school education is by no means confined to the impetus which research has, obviously and immediately, derived from governmental hopes for more effective schooling. She notes a second impetus—'growing reluctance on the part of women to accept the entire responsibility for the care of their young children'—and thus reminds us of the deeper and wider social movements which press upwards on to the surface discussions in the SSRC as a research agency of the state through the underlying political complex which generates definitions and priorities for research. She is conscious, in other words, of those social changes—sexual, occupational and familial as well as educational—to which the political context is itself a complicated response. Accordingly, she takes no narrow or formal view of pre-schooling or of the research which pertains to it. Her catholicity deserves to be underlined. We can usefully distinguish between (formal) education and the more general notion of upbringing: in these terms Dr Tizard can be said to have defined her task as that of reviewing studies of upbringing.

Nothing less was required. What we are witnessing in contemporary society is a new convulsion in the relations between generations or 'the transmission of cultures' which includes a reshaping of the relations between family, state and society at least as fundamental and far-reaching in its implications as the separation of home from work associated with the emergence of primitive industrialism in the eighteenth and nineteenth centuries in Western Europe. The faltering of authority in both the traditional family and the traditional school is a widely recognized and frequently deplored phenomenon which manifests rapid change in that process which sociologists think of as the social reproduction of each new generation. It is on this wider canvas, and not on the narrower view of preparation or compensation or 'headstarting' of those who have yet to enter the formal system of education, that research has to be projected.

The implications are difficult. They challenge the analytical capacities of virtually the whole range of the human sciences. Put briefly, both research workers and their patrons—whether in government departments, research councils or philanthropic foundations—are faced with a dilemma. In order to grasp the significance of questions which are small enough to be manageable within the theories and methods of the established academic disciplines they have to ask large questions which are not. It is characteristic under such circumstances for the research community to seek refuge in a conference attended by scholars representing the whole gamut of social science and psychological fields of enquiry. And again, as a typical outcome there tends to be earnest discussion of the possibilities of interdisciplinary, multi-disciplinary and intersticial collaborative work. Dr Tizard's review was presented to such a conference, organized by the Educational Research Board of the SSRC. I had a strong sense at the conference that the disciplinary participants wanted to guard against 'trained incapacity', their own and even more that of the members of other academic disciplines. At the same time, those who attended were mindful of the range and pace of social movements which press policy-makers towards decision, and hence they were aware of the urgency to establish a firm basis of knowledge and conscious of their responsibility for its adequate translation into advice.

Where, then, are we to take disciplinary grip on the research problems which logically, though not always in practice, are anterior to policy decisions? The most casual reading of Dr Tizard's review demonstrates that a bewildering range of phenomena from the widest 'macro' or collective to the most minute 'micro' or individual are relevant to the understanding of contemporary upbringing. The cognitive worlds in which the different research disciplines of sociology, social anthropology, social psychology and experimental psychology live are all real enough: the problem is to connect them. The phenomena at each of the levels relevant to these disciplines are in rapid flux. At the most macroscopic level, sociological accounts of the changing circumstances of upbringing reveal a metamorphosis of the aims, expectations and conditions of child-rearing. Demographic statistics tell us, for example, that while the population of Britain has risen by half in this century, the grandparental element in it has more than doubled and the number of working women who are wives rose by over 600 per cent between 1911 and 1966. What do these figures indicate about changes in the institutions of reproduction and child-rearing? One optimistic interpretation relates the distributions of fertility and income. Fertility and family size have declined, as have fertility differentials between rich and poor families. Indeed, the *per capita* amounts spent (in both material and psychic terms) on children by both parents and professionals have risen since the war to a point where the shared norm in the reproduction of the next generation is that of a 'quality product'.

On one view, then, we have a cheerful account of 'the century of the child'—a story of increasing affluence and rising norms of child care. Similarly, on a closer view of the character of communities, sociologists and anthropologists have presented a picture of the break-up of analphabetic traditional working-class cultures, increasing occupational, geographical and cultural mobility, widening travel and communication, decreasing hours of work, more equal partnership in marriage, more effective family planning and, not least, a vast development of educational provision and opportunity. And again, looking still more closely at individuals through the eyes of social psychologists we glimpse enlarging self-conceptions and rising expectations among women, infants and members of traditionally disadvantaged social groups, as well as the acceptance of more ambitious goals among professionals and practitioners who work with children.

On the other hand, and again at different levels of aggregation, a more sombre view may be presented. Social control of the circumstances of birth appears to be loosening. The illegitimate birth rate per thousand unmarried women rose from 8.4 in 1901–5 to 19.1 in 1961–65. There is evidence of increasing family breakdown; for example, the number of divorce petitions per 100 marriages contracted annually five to fifteen years earlier was 0.3 in 1911 and 15.9 by 1968 in England and Wales. There are widespread manifestations of professional and pedagogical uncertainty among teachers, paediatricians and social workers of which the demand for research is itself an indicator. There is also evidence of increasing disaffection and alienation among the young; for example, the number of juveniles found guilty of indictable offences rose from 10,786 in 1900 to 63,452 in 1968.

These illustrative social statistics are taken more or less at random from an enormous set. I mention them only to emphasize the lack of an agreed and coherent description of contemporary upbringing even at the broadest societal level. The research task must include production of such a description and one, moreover, which is disaggregated so as to bring smaller social networks more clearly into view—families, play-groups, nursery classes as well as the professional and bureaucratic encounters of children and parents with teachers, nurses, police officers and social workers. The more fundamental research tasks of problem selection and of scientific explanation—whether genetic, psychological or ecological—must remain hazardous in the absence of sophisticated and comprehensive description. There is, in any case and in the crudest sense, an identifiable polarization between 'social' and 'in-dividual' explanations of the behaviour of children, their personalities, their learning and attainments, etc. Equally crudely, it is held that the task is to combine them. How this combination is to be effected is in part a question of how research funding can attend to the organizational terms of fruitful collaboration.

The Organization of research

Hence the interest in searching for new modes of research collabora-tion from which studies of pre-schooling might profit and hence the particular interest in the proposals now being discussed for a centre for educational studies at Oxford which could conceivably provide one creative environment for such a programme of studies. Dr Tizard reports some useful suggestions concerning research organization and including the communication and implementation of research findings. Professor Jack Tizard, for example, has argued for a social science equivalent of the *British Medical Journal* and there is increasing recognition that we lack not only dissemination of findings but adequate arrangements for the mapping and monitoring of research and practice in this field. Again, I would like to supplement what Dr Tizard has to say.

If we take seriously the formulation of pre-schooling problems as a set of issues and ignorances, scientific and administrative, concerning the reproduction of the next generation, it follows that some of the principal hypotheses to be tested must be phrased in life-cycle terms. This in turn suggests longitudinal studies, which are notoriously difficult both theoretically and practically. Theoretically, they frequently suffer from imprisonment within an initial definition of the data to be collected which is inadequate to contain the questions which develop from research experience. Practically, they are difficult to fit into the framework of our conventional methods of funding, of research career patterns and of the established customs of the life-cycle of doctorate research. Pre-schooling is an outstanding example of the general need to invent and maintain research structures with a long—yet nonetheless vigorous—life and to explore the possibilities of bureaucratized data collection in forms which would satisfy the needs of research workers in the social and psychological sciences.

This is not the place to discuss these general issues in all their ramifications. We clearly need both the development of social indicators in order to monitor trends in upbringing and we need organized facilities which would permit the economical testing of theories. Let me cite one among many possible examples. The government already has a General Household Survey and the country also has an administrative system of local education authorities. The question can therefore be raised as to whether it would be possible to extend the GHS and to adapt it to the map of the authorities in such a way as to (1) ensure replicated collection of relevant data on the upbringing of children; (2) provide a sample frame for the identification of theoretically interesting sub-samples (of families, children, educational categories, social groups, etc.) which could then be the object of more intensive study.

Aggregate statistics of the kind I have cited earlier have severe limitations by comparison with the advantages of the individual or household approach to data collection of which the GHS is a potentially valuable example. As my colleagues Keith Hope and Phyllis Thorburn argue, the GHS could be developed as a research resource to provide a variety of techniques relevant to both fundamental research in the academic disciplines and also 'applied' research designed to evaluate policy. For example, on the side of monitoring developments in policy, following the government's announcement of intent to expand nursery provision for particular social groups, it would be possible by means of the GHS schedules to discover whether the children of these groups do in fact attend nursery schools either more than previously or more than the children of other groups. A single item on the schedule repeated at intervals might be sufficient to monitor trends. Aggregate approaches, which involve collecting returns from nursery schools, might appear to yield more conclusive figures but few research workers who are acquainted with the quality of occupational or social information collected in the course of routine administration would place much reliance on such sources. Furthermore, the GHS provides the enormous advantage of permitting the study of correlates of success or failure through its information on various social and economic aspects of a representative sample of families.

The GHS offers the possibility of gathering accurate critical information. Target groups can be contrasted with non-target groups: successes can be contrasted with failures. The nature of the GHS schedules is such that the concomitants of success and failure can also be studied and the credibility of before–after comparisons is secured by well-established institutional control of standards of interviewing, coding, etc. Moreover, although run by a governmental agency (the Office of Population Censuses and Statistics), the Survey organization is not directly interested in the success or failure of any particular social policy.

But still more generally, the research task (as I have phrased it to include the description and explanation of changes in the reproduction of a new generation and including explanation of these processes as well as description of them and evaluation of public policies with respect to them) would be much facilitated if governmental organization for the collection of data could be firmly linked to the research organizations of the academic disciplines so as to provide the latter with accurate measures of trends and changes and a continuous flow of data on families which permitted multivariate analysis of interrelations between adults and children. At all events, we need new methods and new organization if scholars, policy-makers and practitioners are to collaborate effectively in solving problems for themselves and each other.

Educational priority areas

Returning finally to Dr Tizard's references to the EPA programme, I would add two comments. The first is that it is probably both too flattering and too dismissive to label the EPA programme as 'the British equivalent of "Headstart" '. There is a connection, of course: the idea of action-research in EPA districts was a modified outcome of suggestions in the Plowden Report, the authors of which had been attentive to Lyndon Johnson's hopes for a 'Great Society' through educational reform, but the scale of the American investment was vast by comparison with the modest British excursion into five economically and socially deprived districts. Moreover, and on the other hand, we had no excuse for any failure on our part to profit from the American experience. Certainly we had learnt in advance to reject the classic theory which underlies the notion of 'compensatory education', pre-ferring from the outset to think of a theory from which the adjective 'complementary' might more appropriately be deduced. The label is in any case not least alarming when one remembers the now common false knowledge that 'Headstart was a failure'. The uncommonly known truth is much more complicated:[1] if space permits only single-sentence assessments, it must be urged that Headstart was a resounding success. It focused political and social science attention on deprivation in early childhood with unprecedentedly dramatic effectiveness.

The second comment refers to Dr Tizard's discussion of the evidence on 'wash-out' of test gains in which she remarks that 'no assessment was made of the subsequent school attainments of the children who had attended EPA pre-school'. This is not true of the crucial West Riding experiment. In Volume IV of the EPA series (which appeared after Dr Tizard wrote), George Smith reports on two years of primary school testing of those who had attended the EPA pre-schools set up by the project in a situation where there was no previous history of any kind of pre-schooling in the district. Four EPVT scores are now available for these children taken at intervals from 1969 to 1973, the baseline pre-test scores having been taken in March 1969. At the end of the third year in primary school, the average scores were still well above those for comparable groups of children in the 1969 baseline testing, though the gap looked like closing. These trends do not support the suggestion often made, and mentioned by Dr Tizard, that test familiarity explains the differences. The children who attended pre-school seem to trace out the profiles first shown in the baseline testing programme —an initial spurt followed by a gradual decline. But they trace out this pattern at a level well above that found in the 1969 testing. George and Teresa Smith conclude that though the follow-up results can be treated sceptically, the evidence that pre-school work in this case made an impact which has been sustained is difficult to ignore.

It would be rash to make too much of this particular set of findings, which in any case underline Dr Tizard's conclusion that there must be special measures to follow up early help if gains are not to be washed out. On the other hand, we are in no position completely to discard the idea that early schooling has any contribution to make to the avoidance

---

[1] For an authoritative survey of the successes and failures of American education-ally based poverty programmes, see George Smith and Alan Little, *Strategies of Compensation: A Review of Educational Projects for the Disadvantaged in the United States*, OECD, 1971.

of later school failure or the closing of the typical and notorious gaps in achievement between children of different social class origins. The evidence is convincingly strong that there can be no once-and-for-all inoculation in the pre-school years against either individual learning failure or social disadvantage during the school career. But surely there would have to be much more (and more sustained) inquiry into the potentialities of positive discrimination in the context of a wider range of professional and community supports for the family as a learning environment as well as in the setting of imaginative variations in conventional and current modes of formal schooling before we could conclude that education in the early years has no potential effect either on the level of adult competence of individuals or on the inequalities between social groups in the capacity exhibited by their average members to grasp life-chances.

Conclusion

In my view, however, the further exploration of pre-schooling as a set of techniques either for raising educational standards or modifying their social distribution is only one aspect of the wider problem. That wider problem consists of forging a more complete understanding of inter-generational reproduction of culture. To solve it we first need much better description couched in theoretically adequate terms. Meanwhile, we proceed to research and to policy without a map of the territory. We need to measure and then to monitor the trends in both the quantities and qualities of relations between the generations. Is the superficially simple thesis of increasing social segregation of age cohorts true or false? Are the trends secular? Is upbringing being professionalized and if so in what sense? What role is possible for 'amateurs' (mothers, extended kin, neighbours) in modern society? Can we test the more subtle hypothesis that the crisis of upbringing is a function of the relation between subjective expectations ('the quality child') and objective conditions which are improving at a lesser rate?

Description would lay the foundation and new research organizations could facilitate collaborative work on explanation to which a large number of academic specialisms must contribute. The natural laboratory of geographical and social variation within Britain can, of course, be exploited to these ends. Dr Tizard reports a current study of two London boroughs in which fundamental reorganization of public support to child-rearing is under way. We also have the benefit of

Kelmer Pringle's longitudinal study. But we have so far failed to realize the potential for description and analysis which administratively collected data in general and the General Household Survey in particular could provide.

Yet even more adequate national self-study would not suffice to harness the full potential of social scientific analysis. The contemporary revolution of relations between the generations is world-wide. Experimental adaptations of crucial significance are in train in China, Israel, Sweden and elsewhere, while in the United States social scientists like Urie Bronfenbrenner have begun to describe a process of something like chaotic collapse in the traditional order of parent–child relations. This wider natural laboratory also requires our attention. Meanwhile we can revisit the British world of childhood in the 1890s portrayed to us by Arthur Morison in *Child of The Jago* and wonder whether the 'century of the child' has much, if at all, improved the quality of young life.

Nuffield College, Oxford.

FINAL REMARKS BY THE AUTHOR

All of these contributions raise important topics for general debate. I want to comment on only one issue, raised by Halsey, Marion Blank, and Joan Tough in different contexts. That is, the distinction between child-rearing, or upbringing, and education, and the question of the relative contribution which families and formal institutions make to the educational process.

There are real disagreements on this issue, which have important implications for practice, and these disagreements are associated with different meanings given to the term education. Joan Tough defines education as a process 'entrusted to schools . . . through which society intervenes in the life of an individual in order to transmit values, attitudes, skills and knowledge'. In the case of a young child the goals of such a process might include 'moving towards self-control and self-discipline, becoming responsible and reflective, capable of communicating his thinking to others, and having an impetus towards knowing about and understanding the world in which he lives'. Upbringing, on the other hand, is a process which goes on in the home, and which may be more or less compatible with education, since many parents do not accept an 'educational' role, and many of those who do are un-successful in achieving it. The implication of this view is that early childhood education is a job for professionals, and that most young children will not be adequately educated unless they attend nursery school.

To confine the term education to a process that occurs in schools seems, however, very unrealistic, just as it seems very unlikely that the qualities of an 'educated' three-year-old described above could be the outcome of attendance at a morning nursery school. If instead one defines education as any directed effort on the part of one person with the aim that another should acquire skills, bodies of knowledge, attitudes or values, then it is clear that both upbringing and education go on at home and at school. Certainly, much of what a child learns at home is not the result of an educational process, that is, much of his learning results from experiences which have not been planned by an educating adult, or which are the unintended product of planned experiences. This, however, is equally true of school. What the child may learn from an arithmetic lesson is as likely to be a sense of inadequacy or confusion as a numerical skill. Whilst an adult believes he is teaching one thing, the child may well be learning something quite different, and many of the child's basic attitudes and values, for example his concepts of self-identity, class, and sex-role probably result from incidental or unintended learning, rather than from an educational process.

Equally clearly, education is not a process which is confined to school. Much education nowadays occurs through the medium of television; every day large numbers of children watch programmes like *Blue Peter* which have a deliberate educational intent, and are devised not only to impart knowledge but to develop thinking skills. In some families the child's whole environment is arranged with an educational intent—his books, toys, outings, clothes, even his room decorations are chosen with an overt instructional purpose.

It is true the 'invisible curriculum' of families differ. What the mother sees as important to teach her child varies enormously across, and within, social classes, so that many children arrive at primary school ill-prepared for the tasks which confront them. It is not that the child has received no education at home, but rather that some kinds of home education are more appropriate than others for preparing the child for the demands of the primary school. For these children the 'curriculum' of the early years may have to be altered, either by influencing the mother's conception of what she should transmit to the child or by offering supplementary learning experiences outside the home. There is, however, considerable doubt whether the traditional nursery school effectively fulfils this latter function, and a great deal more investigation is needed into what children learn, and what they don't learn, at nursery school. However, the main implication of the broader definition of education is that educationalists need to concern themselves with all the settings in which children are learning. A major concern must be a study of transmission within the home, and the very complex factors which influence this transmission process.

It is because of the implications for practice that I am also unwilling to accept Marion Blank's sharp distinction between upbringing and education. She restricts the term education to attempts by the school to make basic alterations in the child's level of functioning. At the pre-school level she argues that such efforts are only needed for those children in risk of subsequent school failure; for other children, play groups and nursery school need provide only a benign, secure, and interesting environment. This distinction seems to me no more valid than Joan Tough's. All upbringing is likely to involve education in Marion Blank's sense, e.g. any attempt to get a child to see another's point of view, or to assume responsibility for dressing himself, is an attempt to alter his level of functioning.

There are, of course, big differences between families and between different kinds of pre-school institution in the kind of change they try to effect in the child, and the kind of functions they consider important to develop. At the present time, most substitute-care arrangements accept little responsibility for the intellectual development of their charges—at their best, they provide only the secure benign environment described by Marion Blank, and their educational efforts are largely directed to social development, or to achieving a certain standard of obedience, and hygiene. If the home is acting as an effective educational agent in other directions, this deficiency in group care need not be important. But for the children of working mothers—and the number of these is increasing—for five days a week parent–child interaction is likely to be brief and limited to a period when both are tired and probably irritable.

For these children the educational component of the upbringing which they receive in substitute care may be crucial. We have to find ways to bring up children away from their families in such a way that the educational goals which we consider important can be attained. This may be difficult, if only because of the relatively poor ratio of adults to children in most group settings, but a recognition that the process of child-rearing involves education is more likely to lead to better practice than the separation of these roles. If education is seen as a specialized activity, then most adult–child contacts are down-graded to 'child-rearing'. But if education is seen as a pervasive process, then all adult–child contacts are potentially important and fruitful, and nurses, playgroup leaders and childminders should be seen by themselves and by others as offering not only care but education to their charges.

The logic of this argument may seem to deprive the nursery school teacher of her professional role. This should, however, surely be that of a specialist, who because of her greater knowledge of child development and educational techniques is able to help the non-specialists to make their aims explicit, to work out the best methods of attaining them, to help them to assess the success of their attempts, and to innovate new aims herself, and theories and methods. The pedagogy of the early years is as yet relatively undeveloped. We have very little idea of how, by planning, to achieve our educational goals, or how to achieve a better relationship between what the adult teaches and what the child learns; the questions about educational strategy posed by Joan Tough do indeed await answers. For these reasons it seems to me important at a time of expansion of services for under-fives to emphasize the need for innovation, both in the kind of services provided and in educational thinking.

Appendices

Margaret Clark   2, 21, 49, 58, 61, 62, 63, 64, 72,
Department of Psychology   74
Turnbull Building
155 George Street, Glasgow G1 1RD

Alan and Ann Clarke   42, 48, 49, 52, 58, 68, 75, 77
Department of Psychology
The University, Hull

Kevin Connolly   14, 15, 16, 64, 66
University of Sheffield
Department of Psychology
Sheffield S10 2TN

Margaret Donaldson   34, 35, 54, 68, 77
University of Edinburgh
Department of Psychology
60 Pleasance
Edinburgh EH8 9JT

A. H. Halsey (also George Smith,   40, 50, 72, 75
    Teresa Smith, Terry James, Joan
    Payne)
New Barnett House
Little Clarendon Street
Oxford OX1 2ER

Douglas Hubbard   17, 52
The University of Sheffield
Institute of Education
Sheffield S10 2TN

Corinne Hutt   13
Department of Psychology
University of Keele
Staffordshire ST5 7BG

Brian Jackson 22, 40, 53, 59, 60, 69, 70, 73, 75,
National Child Minding Research 77
  and Development Unit
32 Trumpington Street
Cambridge CB2 1QY

Kenneth Jones 8
Redland College
Redland Hill
Bristol BS6 6UZ

Iain Kendell 7
University of Reading
School of Education
London Road
Reading RG1 5AQ

Christopher Kiernan 44, 66, 67, 74, 76, 85
Thomas Coram Research Unit
41 Brunswick Square
London WC1N 1AZ

Margaret Manning 16, 67
University of Edinburgh
Department of Psychology
60 Pleasance
Edinburgh EH8 9JT

Geoffrey Matthews 7, 74
Centre for Science Education
Chelsea College
Bridges Place, London SW6 4HR

Eric Midwinter (also Susan Bell, 20, 50, 70
  Celia Burn, Moira McCrea)
Liverpool Teachers Centre
West Derby Street
Liverpool L7 8TP

Peter Mittler (also Cliff Cunningham, 44, 45, 66
    Dorothy Jeffree, Roy McConky,
    James Hogg, Brian Hopkins, Peter
    Evans)
Hester Adrian Research Centre
The University
Manchester M13 9PL

John and Elizabeth Newson   30, 45, 46, 49, 52, 53
The University of Nottingham
University Park
Nottingham

John Nicholls and Ethel Seaman   19
English Department
Keswick Hall College of Education
Norwich

A. Osborne   37, 80
Child Health and Education in the
    Seventies
University of Bristol, Bristol

Naomi Richman   28
Department of Psychological
    Medicine
Hospital for Sick Children
Great Ormond Street
London WC1 3JH

Martin Richards   30, 31, 68, 70
Unit for Research on Medical
    Applications of Psychology
5 Salisbury Villas, Station Road
Cambridge CB1 2JQ

Nikolas Rose   3, 63
NSPCC
1 Riding House Street
London W1P 8AA

Joanna Ryan 43, 66, 70, 72
Unit for Research on Medical
  Applications of Psychology
5 Salisbury Villas, Station Road
Cambridge CB1 2JQ

Rudolph Schaffer 15, 29
Department of Psvchology
University of Strathclyde
Turnbull Building
155 George Street
Glasgow G1 1RD

Maureen Shields 36, 62, 63, 68
Department of Educational
  Psychology and Child Development
Institute of Education
24 Woburn Square
London WC1

Jack Tizard 41, 42. 53, 54, 62, 67, 71, 72, 75,
Thomas Coram Research Unit 76, 77
41 Brunswick Square
London WC1N 1AZ

Joan Tough viii, 5, 6, 8, 22, 49, 50, 55, 57, 68,
Schools Council Project 74, 76
Institute of Education
The University
Leeds LS2 9JT

Willem Van Der Eyken 38, 39, 50, 52
National Children's Bureau
8 Wakley Street
Islington
London EC1V 7QE

Joyce Watt 38, 50, 52, 63, 64, 65, 67, 71, 74
Department of Education
Kings College

Gordon Wells   24, 25, 55, 75
School of Education Research Unit
University of Bristol
Lyndale House
19 Berkeley Square
Bristol B58 1HE

H. L. Williams   2, 54, 55, 63, 73
NFER
The Mere, Upton Park
Slough, Berkshire

Anthony Wootton   23, 24, 61
Department of Sociology
University of York
Heslington, York YO1 5DD

Peter Wedge   50, 72
National Children's Bureau
8 Wakley Street
Islington
London EC1V 7QE

In addition, discussions were held with:

Maurice Chazan   63, 72
Department of Education
University College of Swansea
Hendrefoilan
Swansea AS2 7N

Alan Davies   63, 64
Linquistics Department
University of Edinburgh

Bryan Dockrell   53, 54, 55, 74, 76
SCRE
16 Moray Place
Edinburgh EH3 6DR

Marianne Parry   51, 52, 65, 67, 70, 73, 74
10 Falcon Close
Westbury-on-Trym
Bristol BS9 3NH

Margaret Roberts   51, 52, 62, 65, 74
10 Woburn Square
London WC1

Philip Williams   53, 59, 75
The Open University
Walton Hall
Milton Keynes MK7 6AA

John Tomlinson   51, 52, 62, 63, 65, 73, 75, 76
Cheshire County Council
County Hall, Chester CH1 1SQ

Henry Nathan   84
OECD
2 Rue Andre Pascal
75775 Paris
France

Alan Brimer   65
University of Bristol
Lyndale House
19 Berkeley Square
Bristol B58 1HE

Tessa Blackstone
Centre for Studies in Social Policy
62 Doughty Street
London WC1N 2LS

Edith Mico
ILEA
Westminster Bridge
London SW1

APPENDIX II   CURRENT RESEARCH PROJECTS

Name of principal investigators	Department	Institution	Title of current research	Date of commencement	Funding body
Prof. B. Bernstein	Sociology Research Unit with Sociology Department	Institute of Education London	Methods for the examination of differences in children's sociolinguistic codings relevant to education	1974	SSRC
Dr N. Blurton-Jones	Dept of Growth & Development, Institute of Child Health	University of London	1 Development of attachment behaviour from ages 1–3	1972	SSRC
			2 The biology and psychology of early mother–child interaction	1975	SSRC
Dr A. Bentley and I Kendell	School of Education	University of Reading	Music education for young children	1970	Schools Council
Prof. J. S. Bruner	Dept of Experimental Psychology	University of Oxford	1 Continuity and discontinuity in the transition from pre-linguistic communication	1974	SSRC
Prof. J. S. Bruner and Dr A. Macfarlane	Dept of Experimental Psychology	University of Oxford	2 The development of interaction patterns in normal and 'at risk' mother–infant pairs		Medical Research Council
Prof. N. Butler and A. Osborne	Dept of Child Health Research Unit	University of Bristol	Child Health & Education in the Seventies	1974	Medical Research Council
Asher Cashdan	Faculty of Educational Studies	Open University	Teaching styles in nursery education	Preliminary work Summer 1973; Pilot study, June 1974	Open University

Researcher	Department	University	Project	Year	Funding
Dr Margaret Clark and Dr Carol Lomax	Dept of Psychology	University of Strathclyde	1 The Dunbartonshire Nursery School Project	1970	Dunbartonshire Education Committee and Scottish Education Department
Dr Margaret Clark and W. Donachy	Dept of Psychology	University of Strathclyde	2 The Renfrewshire Pre-School Project	1973	Scottish Education Department
Prof. A. Clarke and Mrs S. A. Sandon	Dept of Psychology	University of Hull	Experimental programmes for intervention at home with parents of pre-school severely subnormal children	1974	DHSS and Joseph Rowntree Memorial Trust
Prof. Kevin Connolly and Peter K. Smith	Dept of Psychology	University of Sheffield	Determinants of social behaviour in pre-school children	1971	SSRC
Charmian Davie	Dept of Psychology	University of Keele	How pre-school children spend their day	1974	DES
Dr Margaret Donaldson with students 1 Peter Lloyd	Dept of Psychology	University of Edinburgh	1 Verbal communications between pre-school children		None
2 Alison Macrae	Dept of Psychology	University of Edinburgh	2 Language development in young children within the context of cognitive development		University of Edinburgh Studentship 1971/3
3 Lesley Hall	Dept of Psychology	University of Edinburgh	3 A development study of linguistic and perceptual restraints on visual processes		Commonwealth Scholarship
4 Martin Hughes	Dept of Psychology	University of Edinburgh	4 Egocentrism in pre-school children		SSRC

Researcher	Department	Institution	Project	Year	Funder
5 James McGarrigle	Dept of Psychology	University of Edinburgh	5 Language interpretation in studies of cognitive development		MRC
6 Julie Bone	Dept of Psychology	University of Edinburgh	6 Learning of reading by school children and reading difficulties		MRC
7 Louise Lamontagne	Dept of Psychology	University of Edinburgh	7 Dynamic interpretation of static pictures: A study of children's ability to order events in time		Canadian Government
Dr A. H. Halsey and Mrs T. Smith	Dept of Social & Administrative Studies	University of Oxford	Pre-school expansion its impact on parental involvement and on the struction of provision	1974	SSRC
D N. Hubbard	Inst of Education	University of Sheffield	Family needs in the provision of pre-school education	1973	University of Sheffield
Prof. S. J. Hutt and Dr C. Hutt	Psychology Department	University of Keele	Play exploration and learning in the pre-school child	1974	SSRC
Mr Brian Jackson	National Child Minding Research and Developmental Unit		1 Six children from different backgrounds in Huddersfield leave home and start school	1973	SSRC
Brian Jackson and Julia McGawley Sonia Jackson			2 Childminding—A first national inquiry	1973	SSRC
Brian Jackson and Julia McGawley			3 A pilot training course for illegal childminders evaluated	1974	Chase Trust
Brian Jackson and Sonia Jackson			4 A pilot project for raising standards in minders' homes: an evaluation	1974	DHSS
Brian Jackson and Julia McGawley			5 A first experiment in selecting and training day care mothers in Brixton evaluated	1974	Wates Foundation and DHSS
Brian Jackson and Anne Garvey			6 Problems of Chinese children in Britain: a growing minority	1974	Noel Buxton Trust

Name	Centre/Unit	University	Project	Year	Funding
Brian Jackson, Terry Mulrooney, Barrie Knight			7 Educational situation of children of Ugandan refugees	1973	Home Office and Rowntree Trust
Dorothy Jeffree and Roy McConkey	Hester Adrian Research Centre	University of Manchester	1 Parental involvement in facilitating the development of young mentally handicapped children	1973	DHSS & DES
Cliff Cunningham	Hester Adrian Research Centre	University of Manchester	2 Visual skills and reaching behaviour in Down's Syndrome (Mongol) infants	1973	SSRC
Ken Jones	Research Unit, School of Education	Bristol	The use of Rebus materials as 'reading readiness' experience for pre-school children	1973	Research Unit, School of Education, Bristol University
Dr Chris Kiernan	Thomas Coram Research Unit	University of London	The Hornsey intervention project	1973	DHSS
Dr Margaret Manning	Dept of Psychology	University of Edinburgh	A further investigation of patterns of hostility in children	1973	Mental Health Research Fund and SSRC
Prof. G. Matthews and Mrs J. Matthews	Centre for Science Education, Chelsea College	University of London	Early mathematical experiences	1974	Schools Council
Dr E. Midwinter and Susan Bell, Celia Burn, Moira McCrea	Home School Development Unit	Liverpool Teacher Centre	Liverpool parental education programme	1973	Van Leer Foundation
Drs E. Newson J. Newson and Hilary Gray	Child Development Research Unit	University of Nottingham	1 Doctoral study of giving-and-taking behaviour in young babies in the contexts of (a) social play with their mothers and a toy, and (b) non-social presentation of a similar toy	1972	MRC post-grad. grant

Name	Department/Unit	University	Project	Year	Funding
Olwen Jones	Child Development Research Unit	University of Nottingham	2 An analysis of interaction sequences between mothers and pre-verbal mongol infants: a comparative study of mongol and normal children's development of communication skills (doctoral)	1973	MRC post-grad. grant
Susan Packer	Child Development Research Unit	University of Nottingham	3 Development and function of imitation as a means of communication between mothers and their infants (doctoral)	1973	SSRC post-grad. grant
Colin Pryor	Child Development Research Unit	University of Nottingham	4 Parents as behaviour modifiers experiment in parental support, group of parents with young children having a variety of handicaps	1972	MRC grant with additional funds from Mental Health
John Nicholls and Ethel Seaman	English Dept	Keswick Hall College of Education Norwich	The Norwich Feasibility Study: involving parents and teachers	1972	None, relies on volunteers
Dr Martin Richards	Unit for Research on Medical Applications of Psychology	University of Cambridge	Research on child development	1970	Nuffield Foundation
Dr Martin Richards	Unit of Research on Medical Applications of Psychology	University of Cambridge	Mother–infant interaction and its influence on the development of the child	1972	Mental Health Research Fund

Name	Department	Institution	Project title	Year	Funder
Dr Naomi Richman	Dept of Psychological Medicine	Hospital for Sick Children, Great Ormond Street, London	An epidemiological study of the behavioural and developmental problems of young children	1971	DHSS
Nikolas Rose		NSPCC	The effects of playgroup experience on disadvantaged pre-school children	1973	NSPCC and DHSS
Dr Joanna Ryan	Unit for Research on the Medical Application of Psychology	University of Cambridge	A longitudinal study of language development in young severely subnormal children		Nuffield Foundation
Prof. H R Schaffer	Dept of Psychology	University of Strathclyde	1 Studies in socialization processes in infancy	1972	SSRC
Prof. H. R. Schaffer and Prof. T. Markus	Dept of Psychology Dept of Architectures	University of Strathclyde	2 Influence of spatial design factors in nursery schools on the behaviour of children	1973	Scottish Education Department
Mrs M. Shields	Dept of Child Development Institute of Education	University of London	Investigation of the development of language skill in children between 3 and 5 years	1970	SSRC
Prof. J. Tizard	Thomas Coram Research Unit Institute of Education	University of London	Children's Centre research programme	1973	DHSS
Dr Barbara Tizard and	Thomas Coram Research Unit Institute of Education	University of London	Staff and Child behaviour in the pre-school	1971	Dr Barnardo's Society and DHSS
Dr Janet Philps Dr Joan Tough	Institute of Education	University of Leeds	Communication skills in early childhood	1973	Schools Council
W. Van der Eyken	Education Dept (Now at the National Children's Bureau)	Brunel University	Socioeconomic constraints on the public use of community playgroups	1972	SSRC

Dr Joyce Watt	Dept of Education University of Aberdeen	Pre-school education and the family: the relative responsibilities of the local authority services	1973	SSRC and Scottish Education Dept
Peter Wedge and Roy Evans	National Children's Bureau	1 Developmental records project	1972	Dr Barnardo's
		2 Study of pre-school playgroups for children and families in 'high need'	1974	DHSS
		3 Study of evaluation of local authority combined nursery education/day care centres	1974	DHSS/DES
Dr Gordon Wells	Research Unit, School of Education Bristol University of	Language development in pre-school children	1972	SSRC
H. L. Williams	National Foundation for Educational Research, The Mere, Upton Park, Slough	Social handicap and cognitive functioning in pre-school children	1973	National Foundation for Educational Research

Research Projects recently approved by the Department of Education and Science

Prof. J. Hutt and Miss C. Davie	Psychology University of Keele	The experiences of young children at home	1975	DES
Dr R. Sumner	National Foundation for Educational Research, The Mere, Upton Park, Slough	Developing materials for assessment and evaluation	1975	DES
Mr M. Woodhead	National Foundation for Educational Research, The Mere, Upton Park, Slough	The aims, role and development of staff in the nursery	1975	DES

APPENDIX III   REFERENCES

BAIRD, D. and THOMPSON, A. M. (1969) 'Reduction of perinatal mortality by improving standard of obstetric care.' In: BUTLER, N. R. and E. D. ALBERMAN (Eds.) *Perinatal Problems.* Edinburgh: Livingstone.

BERSTEIN, B. (1971) 'On the classification and framing of knowledge.' In: *Class Codes and Control,* Volume I. London: Routledge & Kegan Paul.

BERNSTEIN, B. (1974). 'Class and Pedagogy: visible and invisible.' SRU manuscript in *Class Codes and Control,* Volume III, in press.

BLACKSTONE, T. (1971) A Fair Start: *The Provision of Pre-School Education.* Allen Lane, Penguin, London.

BROWN, G. W. MAIRE NI BHROLCHAIN and TIRRIL HARRIS (in press 1975) 'Social Class and Psychiatric Disturbance among women in an Urban Population,' *Sociology.*

BRUNER, J. S. (1972) *The revelance of education.* London: George Allen & Unwin.

BRYANT, P. (1974) *Perception and Understanding in Young Children.* London: Methuen & Co. Ltd.

COLE, M., GAY, J., CLICK, J. A. R. and SHARP, D. W. (1971) *The Cultural Context of Learning and Thinking. An Exploration in Experimental Anthropology.* London: Methuen & Co. Ltd.

DONALDSON, M. and WALES, R. (1970) 'On the acquisition of some relational terms.' In: J. R. HAYES (Ed.) *Cognition and the development of language.* New York: Wiley.

DONALDSON, M. (1972) 'Preconditions of inference.' In. J. K. COLE (Ed.) *Nebraska Symposium on Motivation 1971.* Lincoln: University of Nebraska Press.

DONALDSON, M. and BALFOUR, G. (1968) 'Less is more: A study of language comprehension in children,' *British Journal of Psychology,* **59**, 461–471.

DONALDSON, M. and LLOYD, P. (1975) 'Sentences and situations: Children's judgements of match and mismatch.' In: F. BRESSON (Ed.) *Les problemes actuels en psycholinguistique.* Paris: CNRS, in press.

DONALDSON, M. and MCGARRIGLE, J. (1975) 'Some clues to the nature of semantic development,' *Journal of Child Language,* in press.

FRANCIS, H. (1974) 'Social Background, Speech and Learning to Read,' *British Journal of Educational Psychology.*

HALSEY, A. H. (1972) *Educational Priority, Vol. 1, EPA Problems and Policies.* London: HMSO.

NATHAN, H. (1973) *Stable Rules: Science and Social Transmission.* Paris: Centre for Educational research and innovation. Organization for Economic Co-operation and Development.

RICHARDS, M. P. M. (Ed.) (1974) Chapter in *The integration of a child into a social world.* Cambridge University Press.

SCHAFFER, H. R. (1974) 'Early Social Behaviour and the Study of Reciprocity,' *Bull Br Psychol Soc,* **27,** 209–216.

SCRIBNER, S. and COLE, M. (1972) *The Cognitive Consequences of Formal and Informal Education.* Address to The American Association for the Advancement of Science, Washington, DC, Dec. 1972.

TIZARD, B., PHILPS, J. and PLEWIS, I. (1975) 'Staff Behaviour in Pre-school Centres,' *J. Child Psychol. Psychiat.* (in press).

TOUGH, J. (1973) 'The Language of Young Children.' In: CHAZAN, M. (Ed). *Education in the Early Years.* University College of Swansea and Aberfan Disaster Fund.

TOUGH, J. (1975) 'Children and Programmes; how shall we educate the young child.' In: DAVIES, A. (Ed.) *Language and Learning in Early Childhood.* Heinemann.

WEIKART, D. P. (1972) Chapter in *Pre-school programmes for the Disadvantaged.* (Ed.) Julian C. Stanley. Baltimore: The Johns Hopkins University Press.

WELLS, G. (1974) 'Learning to Code Experience through Language,' *Child Language,* **1,** 2.

WOOTTON, A. J. (1974) 'Talk in the Homes of Young Children,' *Sociology,* **8,** 2, 277.